Hamlet

WILLIAM SHAKESPEARE

Oxford
Literature
Companions

Notes and activities: Anna Beer
Series consultant: Peter Buckroyd

OXFORD
UNIVERSITY PRESS

Contents

What are Oxford Literature Companions?

Oxford Literature Companions is a series designed to provide you with comprehensive support for popular set texts. You can use the Companion alongside your play, using relevant sections during your studies or using the book as a whole for revision.

Each Companion includes detailed guidance and practical activities on:

- **Plot and Structure**
- **Context**
- **Genre**
- **Characterization and Roles**
- **Language**
- **Themes**
- **Performance**
- **Critical Views**
- **Skills and Practice**

How does this book help with exam preparation?

As well as providing guidance on key areas of the play, throughout this book you will also find 'Upgrade' features. These are tips to help with your exam preparation and performance.

In addition, in the extensive **Skills and Practice** chapter, the 'Exam skills' section provides detailed guidance on areas such as how to prepare for the exam, understanding the question, planning your response and hints for what to do (or not do) in the exam.

In the **Skills and Practice** chapter there is also a bank of **Sample questions** and **Sample answers**. The **Sample answers** are marked and include annotations and a summative comment.

How does this book help with terminology?

Throughout the book, key terms are highlighted in the text and explained on the same page. There is also a detailed **Glossary** at the end of the book that explains, in the context of the play, all the relevant literary terms highlighted in this book.

Which edition of the play has this book used?

Quotations and character names have been taken from the Oxford School Shakespeare edition of *Hamlet* (ISBN 978-0-19-832870-4).

How does this book work?

Each book in the Oxford Literature Companions series follows the same approach and includes the following features:

● **Key quotations** from the play

● **Key terms** explained on the page and linked to a complete glossary at the end of the book

● **Activity boxes** to help improve your understanding of the text

● **Upgrade** tips to help prepare you for your assessment

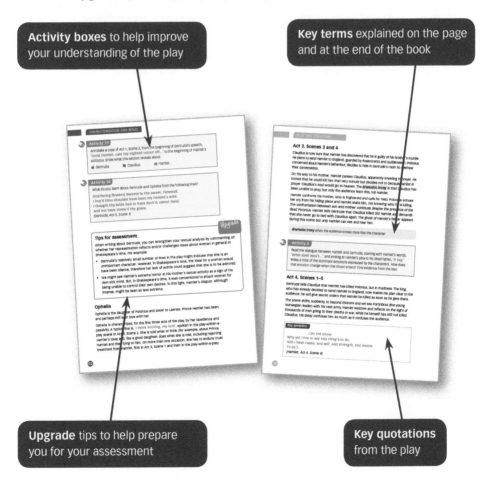

Activity boxes to help improve your understanding of the play

Key terms explained on the page and at the end of the book

Upgrade tips to help prepare you for your assessment

Key quotations from the play

Plot

Act 1, Scene 1

It is night-time on the battlements of the castle of Elsinore in Denmark, a nation threatened by its neighbour Norway and therefore preparing for war. The guards are talking about another crisis, however. The previous night they saw the Ghost of their former king, Hamlet, who has recently died. Now the Ghost comes again, but refuses to speak to them. The guards have invited Horatio, the young prince Hamlet's friend from university, as a witness. They all agree that Hamlet, son of the dead king, should be told about the Ghost, and that perhaps 'This spirit, dumb to us, will speak to him.'

Act 1, Scene 2

Meanwhile, inside the castle, the new king Claudius (the dead king's brother and therefore young Hamlet's uncle) celebrates his recent marriage to young Hamlet's mother, Gertrude. Claudius sends commands to deal with the Norwegian threat.

During this court scene, both Laertes, the son of Claudius's right-hand man Polonius, and young Hamlet want to leave Denmark. Claudius only permits Laertes to go. Hamlet must stay. Hamlet is the only character who is wearing black to show his mourning of the dead king, something his mother Gertrude worries about, asking Hamlet to 'cast thy nighted colour off'. Hamlet talks passionately to her about his powerful but hidden grief for his father, and then has an equally passionate **soliloquy** about his own desire for death ('self-slaughter'). He also expresses his extreme anguish about his mother's hasty marriage to his uncle: 'O most wicked speed!'

Activity 1

Read the first two scenes of *Hamlet*.

a) For each scene, note any key words which describe the atmosphere, setting and use of language. For example, you might write 'dark' or 'chaotic' for the first scene, and 'formal' and 'controlled' for the second scene.

b) Compare your two lists and then write a paragraph summarizing the contrasts between the first two scenes in the play.

---

soliloquy speech by an actor made when he or she is alone on stage, generally reflecting on thoughts and feelings

Tips for assessment

When you are writing about how specific scenes relate to the play as a whole, think of a camera, zooming in on something, but then panning back to show how the detail fits into the whole.

Act 1, Scene 3

Laertes says goodbye to his sister Ophelia, warning her to beware of young Hamlet. The prince has said that he loves Ophelia, but he should not be trusted, according to her brother – an opinion shared by her father Polonius. Polonius gives both his son and daughter long lectures on how they should behave, telling Laertes not to get into trouble in Paris and forbidding Ophelia to talk with Hamlet again.

Act 1, Scenes 4 and 5

Night comes again and the Ghost returns. This time he does speak, but to young Hamlet. The dead king reveals he was murdered by his brother Claudius, who has expressed no repentance. The ghost tells his son he must **'Revenge his foul and most unnatural murder'** *(Act 1, Scene 5)*.

Hamlet swears the guards and his friend Horatio to silence, and tells them he may **'put an antic disposition'** on, presumably so that he will be free to act in strange ways. At this stage of the play, the characters, and the audience, are unsure about the Ghost and his story.

In this 1992 Royal Shakespeare Company production, Kenneth Branagh played Hamlet and Clifford Rose played the Ghost

> **Key quotation**
>
> Thus was I, sleeping, by a brother's hand
> Of life, of crown, of queen at once dispatch'd,
> Cut off even in the blossoms of my sin,
> *(Ghost, Act 1, Scene 5)*

Activity 2

Complete a copy of the table below.

a) Turn the Ghost's words to Hamlet into a list of points, adding more to those already listed.

b) Then find a quotation to illustrate each one.

c) In the final column, highlight which of the Ghost's statements give precise instructions to his son.

What the Ghost is saying	Supporting quotation	Actual instructions
I have to go back to the fires of purgatory soon.	'sulph'rous and tormenting flames' (Act 1, Scene 5)	None
If you ever loved me, revenge my terrible murder.	'Revenge his foul and most unnatural murder' (Act 1, Scene 5)	Unclear how he should revenge the murder
Don't let your mother have sex with your uncle.	'Let not the royal bed of Denmark be / A couch for luxury and damned incest' (Act 1, Scene 5)	

Tips for assessment

When writing about *Hamlet*, it is important to show *how* Shakespeare creates doubts in the audience's minds. For example, this first act opens with a question and Shakespeare builds in many further direct and indirect questions about the status of the Ghost. Uncertainty is created through the language, and you should demonstrate how this happens through close reference to the text.

Act 2, Scenes 1 and 2

The scene shifts back to Polonius and his family. Polonius sets a spy on to his son (who is off to France), and then hears of Hamlet's distressed reaction to Ophelia's rejection of him.

Claudius and Gertrude are also concerned by Hamlet's behaviour and have summoned two of his university friends, Rosencrantz and Guildenstern, to Denmark to try to find out why he is acting so strangely.

In the middle of this, news comes that Norway is no longer a threat. Instead of invading Denmark, young Fortinbras, the Norwegian leader, now simply asks to be allowed to pass through the country with his army.

Polonius suggests engineering a meeting between Ophelia and Hamlet in order to find out the truth about his strange behaviour. Claudius jumps at the idea. Polonius, and then Rosencrantz and Guildenstern, try to find out from Hamlet what is wrong with him, but he is suspicious and gives nothing away.

A theatre troupe arrives and the Players are warmly welcomed by Hamlet. He secretly asks the lead actor to add a few extra lines into their performance, which will take place later that night. Hamlet fears that the Ghost he has seen might be a devil, and so wants proof that Claudius is guilty. Hamlet thinks that, if Claudius sees a play that represents the circumstances of the death of the old King Hamlet, the way he reacts will reveal whether he was guilty of the murder or not.

> **Key quotation**
>
> The spirit that I have seen
> May be a devil, and the devil hath power
> T'assume a pleasing shape, yea, and perhaps,
> Out of my weakness and my melancholy,
> As he is very potent with such spirits,
> Abuses me to damn me.
> *(Hamlet, Act 2, Scene 2)*

Activity 3

In Act 2, Scene 2, Hamlet says that Denmark is a prison. From the text, identify three ways in which Denmark can be seen as a prison.

Act 3, Scene 1

Rosencrantz and Guildenstern report to Claudius that Hamlet has refused to confide in them. Claudius and Polonius carry out their plan of spying on Hamlet and Ophelia. Hamlet rejects Ophelia brutally and Claudius is now convinced that his nephew is not mad for love, but for some other reason. It is uncertain whether Hamlet knows that he is being watched or not.

Act 3, Scene 2

Hamlet lectures the Players on the art of acting. The Players then perform their play, called 'The Mousetrap', written by Hamlet. At the critical moment (when poison is poured into a sleeping character's ear), Claudius leaps up, calling for lights and stopping the performance. Hamlet is now certain of his uncle's guilt.

Rosencrantz and Guildenstern arrive to summon Hamlet to his mother's room. He makes it clear to them that he knows what they are trying to do and that they won't succeed. As Hamlet says, **'though you fret me, you cannot play upon me'**.

Act 3, Scenes 3 and 4

Claudius is now sure that Hamlet has discovered that he is guilty of his brother's murder. He plans to send Hamlet to England, guarded by Rosencrantz and Guildenstern. Polonius, concerned about Hamlet's behaviour, decides to hide in Gertrude's room to overhear their conversation.

On his way to his mother, Hamlet passes Claudius, apparently kneeling in prayer. He knows that he could kill him that very minute but decides not to because whilst in prayer Claudius's soul would go to heaven. The **dramatic irony** is that Claudius has been unable to pray, but only the audience learn this, not Hamlet.

Hamlet confronts his mother, who is frightened and calls for help. Polonius echoes her cry from his hiding place and Hamlet stabs him, not knowing who he is killing. The confrontation between son and mother continues despite the presence of the dead Polonius. Hamlet tells Gertrude that Claudius killed Old Hamlet and demands that she never go to bed with Claudius again. The ghost of Hamlet's father appears during this scene but only Hamlet can see and hear him.

> **dramatic irony** when the audience knows more than the character

Activity 4

Read the dialogue between Hamlet and Gertrude, starting with Hamlet's words, **'What devil was't...'** and ending at Hamlet's plea to his dead father, **'O say.'** Make a note of the dominant emotions expressed by the characters. How does that emotion change when the Ghost enters? Find evidence from the text.

Act 4, Scenes 1–5

Gertrude tells Claudius that Hamlet has killed Polonius, but in madness. The king, who has already decided to send Hamlet to England, now makes his plan clear to the audience: he will give secret orders that Hamlet be killed as soon as he gets there.

The scene shifts, suddenly, to beyond Elsinore and we see Fortinbras (the young Norwegian leader) with his vast army. Hamlet watches and reflects on the sight of thousands of men going to their deaths in war, while he himself has still not killed Claudius. His delay confuses him as much as it confuses the audience.

> **Key quotation**
>
>   I do not know
> Why yet I live to say this thing's to do,
> Sith I have cause, and will, and strength, and means
> To do't.
> *(Hamlet, Act 4, Scene 4)*

The action of the play returns to the castle and the collateral damage from Polonius's death: the madness of his daughter Ophelia.

Her brother Laertes, who has returned from Paris at the news of his father's killing, bursts in, threatening Claudius. Laertes believes Claudius is guilty of the murder. The king calms Laertes, who is then devastated by the sight of his sister's distressed state.

Activity 5

a) List the kinds of things Ophelia sings about in her madness.

b) Do you agree with Claudius's assessment that Ophelia's madness is **'the poison of deep grief: it springs / All from her father's death'**? Can you suggest other reasons for her madness? Find evidence for your answers.

Act 4, Scenes 6 and 7

Another sudden shift follows and we learn that Hamlet has turned the tables on Claudius, switching letters on board the ship taking him to England. His one-time friends from university will be killed on arrival there, not him.

The news of Hamlet's return to Denmark shocks Claudius, who decides that he will use Laertes to eliminate Hamlet. Laertes is already fired up with the desire to revenge Polonius's death. The king sets up a fencing match between the two young men. Laertes's foil (sword) will be poisoned, but Claudius also plans to poison the wine that Hamlet will be offered.

News comes of the death of Ophelia, by drowning.

Act 5, Scene 1

We see the preparations for Ophelia's burial. As the two gravediggers chat and sing, Hamlet and Horatio arrive and join the conversation. However, when Hamlet realizes who it is that is to be buried, he jumps into the grave and claims he loved Ophelia far more than her brother Laertes did.

> **Key quotation**
>
> I lov'd Ophelia. Forty thousand brothers
> Could not with all their quantity of love
> Make up my sum.
> (Hamlet)

Activity 6

By setting this scene in a graveyard and giving Hamlet a dialogue with a gravedigger, how does Shakespeare show us that Hamlet has changed?

Act 5, Scene 2

Hamlet and Laertes begin their fencing match. Within minutes, there is carnage. Laertes does succeed in wounding Hamlet with his poisoned sword, but is himself poisoned because the two men exchange weapons. The king, who has poisoned the wine intended for Hamlet, sees his queen Gertrude toast her son and drink from the poisoned cup. As Gertrude falls, Hamlet finally turns on his uncle and stabs him, forcing him then to drink his own poison.

With his dying breath, Hamlet asks Horatio to tell his story, but also gives his 'voice' (political support) to Fortinbras of Norway, who arrives at just that moment to see the entire royal family of Denmark dead. Fortinbras takes the throne.

Structure

At its simplest, the plot is the story of the play, that is, 'what happens' in *Hamlet*. However, our understanding of the plot cannot be separated from the *way* in which the story is told, and, in particular, the play's structure.

The play is divided up into five acts. Each act has a particular function in the overall structure of the play.

Act 1

Act 1 introduces the main characters and sets up the conflict that will drive the play.

In *Hamlet*, the appearance of the Ghost is the most significant driver of the action to come, but there are two other sources of dramatic conflict outlined to the audience:

- the threat of invasion from Norway
- the relationship between Ophelia and Hamlet.

Activity 7

Read Act 1, Scene 3. Then do *one* of the following:

- As Ophelia: write to a friend, saying what has been happening between you and Hamlet; how your brother and father see the relationship; and how you see it going forward.

- As Laertes: write to a friend about your sister's relationship with Hamlet and why you think your advice to her is right.

Act 2

Having set up the three conflicts, Shakespeare slows things down in Act 2.

The only significant development is the arrival of the Players, although we learn that the threat of invasion is over, which closes down one plot line. Act 2 slows down still further when the Players run through some very long speeches.

If you focus on character rather than plot, however, Act 2 complicates the issues that have been set up in Act 1. Most importantly, the audience is uncertain about Hamlet's sanity. He speaks first with Polonius, and then with Rosencrantz and Guildenstern. All three of them are determined to find out the cause of his madness, but all three remain as unsure as the audience are about Hamlet's state of mind.

Activity 8

Hamlet makes a plan at the end of Act 2.

Focusing on the final lines of his soliloquy (starting at **'Hum – I have heard...'** *(Act 2, Scene 2)*), work out:

- what Hamlet intends to do
- what he hopes to get out of it
- the reasons behind his plan.

Key quotations

Though this be madness, yet there is method in't.
(Polonius, Act 2, Scene 2)

> **The play's the thing**
Wherein I'll catch the conscience of the king.
(Hamlet, Act 2, Scene 2)

Act 3

Before Hamlet puts the plan into action, Shakespeare slows things down again. He creates scenes in which Hamlet lectures the actors on how to act, tells Horatio his ideas about life, and publicly humiliates Ophelia with his crude jokes and behaviour before the performance of 'The Mousetrap', e.g. **'Lady, shall I lie in your lap?'** *(Act 3, Scene 2)*

Hamlet (Ralph Fiennes) humiliates Ophelia (Tara Fitzgerald) at the play in a 1995 production at the Hackney Empire, London

Activity 9

Draw up a timeline, showing Hamlet's actions immediately after 'The Mousetrap'.

Act 4

After a very busy, even chaotic, start to Act 4, where the audience hears Claudius authorize the death of Hamlet, and sees Fortinbras and his army, the pace of the action slows again. The scenes which follow focus on Ophelia's madness and the quiet moment when Gertrude describes the girl's death.

The act ends with Laertes weeping, but also vowing to take violent action to avenge the death of his father and sister.

Act 5

The final act begins with a long and often darkly humorous scene involving the gravediggers, who are joined by Hamlet and Horatio. This is the calm before the storm. There follows a melodramatic encounter between Hamlet and Laertes, who fight in Ophelia's grave.

Yet again, however, Shakespeare delays the **denouement**. The audience knows that Claudius (having failed to have Hamlet killed in England) is going to use Laertes to kill him in the fencing match, but still we have to sit through some banter between Hamlet and the courtier Osric before, at last, we reach the dramatic **climax** of the play.

Freytag's pyramid

In the 19th century, a German novelist called Gustav Freytag developed a model of dramatic structure. This is often used as a way to represent and analyse the standard five-act structure of plays. At its simplest, it can be represented in this diagram. This model is a useful way of analysing the structure of *Hamlet*.

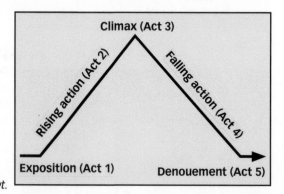

climax the point in a literary work in which the tension reaches its highest point

denouement resolution of the conflicts represented in a literary work

exposition introduction of events, settings and characters to the audience

falling action sequence of events after the climax but before the resolution

rising action series of incidents that create tension and interest for the audience

The ending of *Hamlet*

In performance, it can be difficult for the audience to follow what is going on in the final scene of *Hamlet* because everything happens very quickly. The final minutes of the play pass in a blur of violence and death. For some, the ending is unsatisfactory precisely because it is chaotic. For others, it is completely satisfactory because it *is* chaotic. Hamlet doesn't carry out a careful plan to kill Claudius. He simply seizes his moment.

Shakespeare uses Horatio to sum up the play in the final moments. Horatio tries to explain to Fortinbras why he has walked into a scene of havoc, with 'so many princes' lying dead (*Fortinbras, Act 5, Scene 2*).

Activity 10

Add annotations to a copy of the following speech, with examples of the things that Horatio says have happened in Elsinore. One annotation has been added for you.

> the marriage of Gertrude and Claudius

> So shall you hear
> Of **carnal**, bloody, and unnatural acts,
> Of accidental judgments, casual slaughters,
> Of deaths put on by cunning and forc'd cause,
> And, in this upshot, purposes mistook
> Fall'n on the inventors' heads.
> (*Horatio, Act 5, Scene 2*)

Tragic form

Another way of thinking about *Hamlet* is to see the play in terms of the structure of a **tragedy**. In a conventionally structured tragedy, the following occur over the course of five acts:

- At the start, something occurs that disrupts the normal order of things.
- Chaos and disorder in society results.
- Extreme emotions are involved.
- Social restraint disintegrates.
- Order is restored.

Activity 11

To what extent do you think that 'order is restored' at the end of *Hamlet*, as in the standard structure of a tragedy? Find evidence from the last scene of the play to support your answer.

tragedy a serious work (usually a play) in which the main character becomes involved in conflict with disastrous results and the course of events is usually presented as inevitable

Tips for assessment

When writing about events in the play, consider carefully how characters describe what has happened. There might be a reason that what a character says may not match our experience of the play. For example, at the end of *Hamlet*, Horatio speaks very publicly to Fortinbras, giving the official version of what has happened.

Plot and subplot

There are three plots in *Hamlet*: the main plot and two **subplots**, which echo themes explored in the main plot. These subplots contribute to the overall effect of the play, but do not detract from the main plot.

> **subplot** a secondary plot (storyline) that runs alongside and supports the main plot

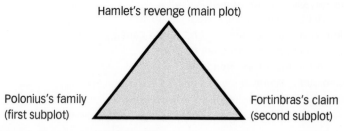

Main plot

The main plot is centred on revenge. Hamlet needs to decide whether he should, and then work out how, he will revenge himself on his uncle, who has killed his father.

First subplot

This involves the family of Polonius. Some see the most important element to this subplot as the breakdown of the relationship between Hamlet and Ophelia, whilst others see the character of Laertes as significant, in that he too has a father killed. Laertes therefore acts as a direct parallel and contrast to the character of Hamlet.

Second subplot

This has its roots in the past, but also has a connection with revenge and with fathers. Old Hamlet previously killed Old Norway (the father of young Fortinbras) in single combat and won some of his land. Now young Fortinbras wants that land back, **'by strong hand'** *(Act 1, Scene 1)*. This is why the guards are keeping such careful watch at the beginning of the play. Indeed, Horatio believes the Ghost is a sign that war will come soon: the **'precurse of fear'd events'** *(Act 1, Scene 1)*. In Act 1, Scene 2, Claudius reveals that young Fortinbras is acting without the permission or knowledge of his uncle, the king of Norway. Claudius sends his ambassadors to Norway to ask that young Fortinbras be stopped. They return, in Act 2, to report success: the Norwegians will **'never more'** attack Claudius *(Act 2, Scene 2)*. Instead, Fortinbras will take his army to Poland.

Shakespeare brings his plots together at key moments. Hamlet, on his way to exile in England in Act 4, meets a captain in Fortinbras's army. They are, as promised, on their way to Poland. The war is revealed, however, as completely meaningless: thousands of men are going to fight for a little patch of ground (Act 4, Scene 4) which is of no value.

The war might be pointless, but, in the context of the play, the moment is important because it prompts Hamlet's final soliloquy, as he thinks about Fortinbras's apparent willingness to go to war, and take twenty thousand men to their deaths, over something so insignificant. In other words, it brings us back to the main plot, Hamlet's revenge.

> **Key quotation**
>
> to my shame I see
> **The imminent death of twenty thousand men**
> **That, for a fantasy and trick of fame,**
> **Go to their graves like beds**
> *(Hamlet, Act 4, Scene 4)*

Fortinbras returns in the last few minutes of the play and Hamlet gives the Norwegian prince his **'dying voice'** *(Act 5, Scene 2)*. Fortinbras has the final lines of the play.

Activity 12

The Fortinbras plot is set up in Act 1, Scene 2. When does it reappear in the play again? What is the dramatic effect of leaving such a long gap?

Activity 13

Make a copy of the diagram below. Draw arrows to link the three plots and add annotations to explain the links.

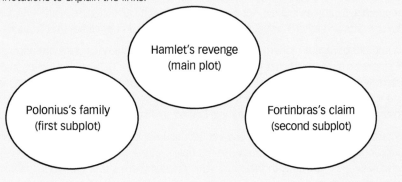

Hamlet's revenge
(main plot)

Polonius's family
(first subplot)

Fortinbras's claim
(second subplot)

Settings

Shakespeare sets almost all of the action in *Hamlet* in or around the castle of Elsinore in Denmark. He makes the settings for his play important to the characters and the action. For example, the graveyard is the place where Hamlet is able to remember the dead and to talk about death. This is in sharp contrast to the court, where he is told from the opening scenes not to 'for ever with thy vailed lids / Seek for thy noble father in the dust' *(Act 1, Scene 2)*, and that 'all that lives must die'. By placing Hamlet in a graveyard, and giving him a dialogue with a gravedigger, Shakespeare shows us how Hamlet has changed on his return to Denmark.

Kronberg Castle, Denmark, which some believe to be Shakespeare's inspiration for Elsinore, the setting for *Hamlet*

Within Elsinore, Shakespeare contrasts very public settings (such as Act 1, Scene 2 and the final scene of the play, when the stage would be crowded with people) with private settings (such as the **closet** scene, between Gertrude and Hamlet, and the 'rash intruder' Polonius).

> **closet** bedroom or private room

Both Hamlet and Laertes begin the play wanting to get away from Elsinore, respectively back to university at Wittenburg and to city life in Paris. This is, in part, because, as Hamlet says to Rosencrantz and Guildenstern, 'Denmark's a prison' *(Act 2, Scene 2)*.

Shakespeare creates a world in which spying is normal, even in the most private of moments. Examples include Act 3, Scene 1, in which Ophelia gives Hamlet back his lover's gifts and when Hamlet speaks with his mother in her closet *(Act 3, Scene 4)*.

A number of recent modern-dress film and theatre productions draw attention to Elsinore as a place of constant surveillance. In a National Theatre production in 2010, starring Rory Kinnear, for example, the designer created 'a claustrophobic panelled set with many halls and windows, so that in every scene, men wearing suits with ear pieces and wrist microphones lurk like Secret Service men bent on no good'.

Shakespeare moves the action outside the castle at key moments and also refers to locations far away from Denmark. He not only creates a sense of a wider world, but also sets up contrasts with the court, which reveal more about the world in which Hamlet has to operate.

Activity 14

Create a very rough map of the world of *Hamlet*, with the castle of Elsinore at its centre (complete with Ophelia's and Gertrude's closets, and battlements), and around it the other settings for the play (the graveyard, England, France, Norway). Make a note of one thing that happens in each setting.

Activity 15

Read the following lines carefully, taking note of the dramatic context and setting in which they are said.

- **How dangerous is it that this man goes loose! / Yet must not we put the strong law on him: / He's lov'd of the distracted multitude** (*Act 4, Scene 3*)

- **Go softly on.** (*Act 4, Scene 4*)

- **Truly to speak [....] but the name.** (*Act 4, Scene 4*)

- **They cry, 'Choose we! [...] Laertes king.'** (*Act 4, Scene 5*)

What do these lines tell you about the world *outside* the castle of Elsinore? Write a short paragraph summarizing what the play as a whole gains and loses by directly, or indirectly, showing us a world beyond Elsinore. Explain why.

The rules of tragedy

Hamlet is described as a tragedy (see page 32). The use of different settings is one of the ways in which Shakespeare breaks the theoretical structural 'rules' of tragedy. One of the great theorists of tragedy, the ancient Greek writer Aristotle (384–322 BC) argued that a play should obey three 'unities':

- time (the action should occur over a period of no more than 24 hours)
- place (the stage should not represent more than one place)
- action (there should be one central plot, with minimal subplots).

Shakespeare may ignore most of Aristotle's rules of tragedy, but he creates a sense of unity in different ways of structuring *Hamlet*. One way he does this is through his use of language (see pages 58–69).

Activity 16

To what extent does Shakespeare follow Aristotle's rules of tragedy in the structure of *Hamlet*?

Foils

In *Hamlet*, Shakespeare encourages the audience to compare and contrast characters who have things in common, with the less important character acting as a **foil** to the main character. Often, the contrast allows us to understand the main character more fully. For example, Ophelia, like Hamlet, Laertes and Fortinbras, loses her father. There is, however, an even more important way in which she acts as a foil to the character of Hamlet – in her madness. Through the character of an unnamed 'Gentleman', Shakespeare provides detailed information to the actor playing Ophelia on how to show her insanity.

> **Key quotation**
>
> **She speaks much of her father, says she hears**
> **There's tricks i'th' world, and hems, and beats her heart,**
> **Spurns enviously at straws, speaks things in doubt**
> **That carry but half sense.**
> *(Gentleman, Act 4, Scene 5)*

Hamlet says he will *perform* madness, and does so, teasing Polonius (**'You are a fishmonger'**) in Act 2, Scene 2 or taunting Claudius (**'Farewell, dear mother'**) in Act 4, Scene 3, when he finally reveals the location of Polonius's body. But, as the audience sees, Ophelia does not *perform* madness. She really is mad.

Another parallel in the play is between Claudius and Old Hamlet. It is a parallel that Hamlet himself is very aware of. In his first soliloquy, in Act 1, Scene 2, he describes his father as **'So excellent a king, that was to this / Hyperion to a satyr'**. For Hamlet, his father is like the glorious sun-god Hyperion and Claudius is like a satyr, half-man, half-beast and controlled by his lust.

Activity 17

Complete a copy of the table below to show where a character has each experience or characteristic listed.

	Hamlet	Laertes	Fortinbras
Father is killed			
Loves Ophelia			
Violent			
Thoughtful			
Inspired by revenge			

Activity 18

What, for you, is revealed about Hamlet when he is contrasted with:

- Laertes?
- Fortinbras?

Provide evidence from the text in your answer.

This **doubling** of characters is also reflected in the play's language. There is a lot of repetition of words and phrases (**'Rest, rest, perturbed spirit'** in *Act 1, Scene 5* is just one example). Shakespeare uses phrases with the word 'and' over 250 times during the play. Often, two words are used when one would do: e.g. **'book and volume'** *(Hamlet, Act 1, Scene 5)*; **'native and indued'** *(Gertrude talking of Ophelia's death, Act 4, Scene 7).*

Doubling occurs at the level of plot, character and language. Using two words (when one would be enough) not only contributes to the length of the play, but also adds to the audience's experience of delay and uncertainty. This is another example of how the structure of the play contributes to the themes.

> **doubling** in the theatre, when one actor plays two parts (e.g. in *Hamlet*, the actor playing the Ghost often also plays Claudius); in literary criticism, the many different kinds of dualism or doubleness, whether in plot, character or language
>
> **foil** a character who contrasts and parallels the main character in a play or story

Writing about structure

A structural technique may take many different forms and it is good to show awareness of a variety of these, whether the technique is visible in language, form or characterization. For example, Shakespeare's use of foils, or parallels, is just one of the ways in which he uses doubling in his play. Others include the presence of two guards at the start of the play and the creation of two pairs of interchangeable characters (Rosencrantz and Guildenstern, and Cornelius and Voltemand). And, of course, there are two kings and two revengers. As the critic Tony Tanner wrote, 'In a word, there seem to be two of everything' in *Hamlet*.

Biography of William Shakespeare

- Shakespeare was born in April 1564 in Stratford-upon-Avon, in Warwickshire.

- He was educated at the King's Free Grammar School in Stratford.

- He married Anne Hathaway in November 1582, when he was 18 years old, and the couple's first child, Susannah, was born six months later.

- In 1585, William and Anne became parents of twins, a boy (Hamnet) and a girl (Judith). Hamnet died when he was only 11 years old. It is thought that Shakespeare left Stratford, and therefore his wife and children, to pursue a career in the theatre.

- Shakespeare became known as an actor and playwright in London in the 1590s. His early works were history plays. He was successful enough to buy the second-largest house in Stratford-upon-Avon for the sum of £60.

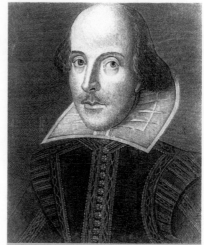

Little is known about Shakespeare's life, but it is thought that *Hamlet* was written in around 1600

- From at least the mid-1590s, he was a member of the Lord Chamberlain's Men, one of the most successful theatre companies of the time. They were often invited to perform at court and, when the Globe Theatre opened in 1599, it became their main public theatre venue.

- The Globe Theatre could hold up to 3,000 spectators and was the most magnificent venue London had ever seen. A star performer was Richard Burbage, the most famous actor of his time, who was the first actor to play Hamlet.

- *Hamlet* was first printed in 1603, the same year in which Queen Elizabeth I died, but it was probably first performed in 1601. The 1603 edition is known as the Bad Quarto, being shorter and less sophisticated than the later versions. It is possible that it was a version designed for acting companies that travelled round the country, and even overseas, to perform the latest plays. King James VI of Scotland, who succeeded Queen Elizabeth I, supported Shakespeare's company, re-naming it the King's Men.

- After continuing to be successful, professionally, for another ten years, Shakespeare retired to Stratford-upon-Avon around 1613.

- William Shakespeare made his will on 26 March and died less than a month later on 23 April 1616.

- *Hamlet* continued to be popular through the centuries, not least with royal audiences. Court records show that it was performed for King James I in 1619 and for King Charles I in 1637.

The English Renaissance

Shakespeare was writing in what is known as the English Renaissance. The Renaissance began in Italy some two hundred years before Shakespeare's time, when the works of the Greek and Roman writers were discovered, and the arts, literature and philosophy were revitalized. The Renaissance may have come late to England but, during Shakespeare's lifetime, literature (especially theatre and poetry) and the arts (especially music and portraiture) flourished.

Tips for assessment

You should only mention details of Shakespeare's life in relation to how they may have influenced the writing or performance of *Hamlet*. Very little is known about Shakespeare's life, so it is advisable to comment on general historical context, rather than on his individual experience.

Activity 1

a) Read through the information about Shakespeare presented here. What, for you, is the most important political change that occurs around the time of the writing, performance and publication of *Hamlet*?

b) What, for you, is the most important change in the theatre world?

c) What links, if any, can you make between your two answers and the plot, themes or characters in *Hamlet*?

Revenge in Shakespeare's time

Most of us know what it is like to want revenge, but few of us take it into our own hands to carry out. In many cases that is because once we are calm, we realize the moral truth that two wrongs don't make a right – an eye for an eye makes the whole world blind. Alternatively, it is because we believe that justice will be enforced by others, for example, by the police and legal system.

In Shakespeare's time, the main reasons *not* to take revenge were found in the Bible. Two references are particularly important. '"It is mine to avenge […]" says the Lord' *(Romans 12: 19)* makes clear that revenge should be, and would be, handled by God, rather than humans. 'But I tell you, do not resist an evil person. If anyone slaps you on the right cheek, turn to them the other cheek also' *(Matthew 5: 39)* is the famous instruction from Jesus, often paraphrased as 'turn the other cheek'. This does not tell us simply to ignore an injury, but to offer oneself for further injury. It is clear that the Church taught that taking revenge into one's own hands was a sin (an immoral act, considered to be against divine law) and therefore against the word of God. The political authorities also maintained that revenge outside the law was a crime.

That is all very well in theory, but the question remains: What should be the individual's response to evil in the world? It is not easy to turn the other cheek. What is more, there was still a powerful tradition alive in Shakespeare's time whereby personal revenge could, and should, be carried out if a member of one's family was injured. We can see echoes of this in so-called 'honour killings' today. Revenge for an injury to one's family could, therefore, be seen as a duty. Moreover, the desire for revenge was certainly seen as a natural reaction.

To complicate things further, if someone was determined to avenge an injustice, it was possible then, as now, to put together a religious justification for one's action. The revenger might consider himself or herself to be an instrument of divine vengeance, believing that God is acting through them and therefore responsible for their actions.

Revenge was a particularly hot topic in Shakespeare's time. One of the most popular plays of the time was Thomas Kyd's *The Spanish Tragedy*, first performed in the late 1580s, more than ten years before *Hamlet* was written. One of the reasons *The Spanish Tragedy* was so popular is that it dramatized revenge, which was something that was concerning people in Shakespeare's England, but set it safely at a distance in Spain.

Key quotation

Let come what comes, only I'll be reveng'd
Most throughly for my father.
(Laertes, Act 4, Scene 5)

Activity 2

Look at the news and find a recent story that involves revenge. Discuss it with others. Do you understand and/or sympathize with the revenger's motives?

Activity 3

Read the following passage, written soon after Shakespeare's death, by his contemporary, Francis Bacon. Using the ideas in the passage, explain in modern language why it is wrong to take revenge.

 Revenge is a kind of wild justice; which the more man's nature runs to, the more ought law to weed it out. For as for the first wrong, it doth but offend the law; but the revenge of that wrong pulleth the law out of office. Certainly, in taking revenge, a man is but even with his enemy; but in passing it over, he is superior.

(Francis Bacon, 'On Revenge')

Tips for assessment

When writing about the representation of Hamlet and his revenge, mention the literary and historical context only when it helps explain or explore Shakespeare's dramatic choices. For example, you might make the following points:

- At the end of revenge tragedies, the convention was for the revenge hero to die once he (and occasionally she) had achieved revenge. For audiences in Shakespeare's time, it was too shocking – morally, politically and theatrically – for the revenger to be rewarded for taking revenge into their own hands.

- In Shakespeare's sources, the revenger Hamlet is successful, survives and becomes king. This is one example of how following the dramatic conventions of his time was more important to Shakespeare when writing *Hamlet* than being faithful to his sources.

Ghosts, Heaven and Hell

Shakespeare was writing about ghosts at a time when Christian attitudes and beliefs were changing. England had become a Protestant country only a generation before Shakespeare's birth. Prior to that it had been Catholic. (Protestantism and Catholicism are both forms of Christianity.)

Protestants and Catholics have different beliefs about the after-life. Protestants in Shakespeare's time believed that when someone died, their soul went straight to either Heaven or Hell for eternity and therefore they could not return as a ghost. In Shakespeare's time, the threat of Hell and everlasting damnation was very real for most people.

However, Catholics believed that the dead went to Purgatory if they had not made full confession of their sins. Purgatory offered people the chance to purge the sins they had committed

Detail of *Purgatory* as painted by Hieronymus Bosch, 1450–1516

in their lifetime and the length of time spent there depended on how sinful they had been. It was seen as preferable to an eternity in Hell. Shakespeare refers to this Catholic belief with the possibility that a spirit in Purgatory might be able to 'walk the night', returning to the human world during the hours of darkness, as the Ghost himself explains in Act 1, Scene 5.

The beliefs that underpin the presentation of Shakespeare's Ghost in *Hamlet* had, officially at least, been swept away in the English Reformation of the 1530s. King Henry VIII had created a national Protestant Church in England and rejected the authority of the Catholic Church and its leader, the pope. To a Protestant audience in the early 1600s, a ghost was likely to be a figment of the viewer's imagination, created by the Devil.

As one social historian, Keith Thomas, wrote, 'Despite the truth of the tale the Ghost had to tell, every firm Protestant in the audience would have been justified in regarding the apparition [ghost or vision] as a devil in human form'. The Devil was generally believed to prey upon the weak – women, children and those who were depressed or melancholic. Hamlet himself makes reference to this in his soliloquy at the end of Act 2.

Key quotations

I am thy father's spirit,
Doom'd for a certain term to walk the night,
And for the day confin'd to fast in fires,
Till the foul crimes done in my days of nature
Are burnt and purg'd away.
(Ghost, Act 1, Scene 5)

It is a damned ghost that we have seen,
And my imaginations are as foul
As Vulcan's stithy.
(Hamlet, Act 3, Scene 2)

Activity 4

Read Hamlet's words about the Ghost in Act 2, Scene 2, from **'The spirit that I have seen'** to the end of his soliloquy. What do they reveal about:

- the attitudes in Shakespeare's time towards ghosts?
- the character of Hamlet?

Suicide

Christian doctrine in Shakespeare's time held that suicide was a mortal sin (a wicked act leading to damnation). To kill yourself meant that you despaired of God's mercy. It was for this reason that a suicide would not be allowed a Christian burial, but be buried at a crossroads instead. This was one way of showing that the person had lost their way in life.

However, writers of the Greek and Roman classical period, who had been rediscovered in the Renaissance, represented suicide as a noble and courageous act. They created characters who ended their own lives rather than face dishonour, and who were praised for their actions. Shakespeare explores these issues in his play *Julius Caesar*, first performed in 1599, close in time to the writing of *Hamlet*. They are also referred to in the very last scene of *Hamlet*.

These beliefs are also important in helping to understand Hamlet's attitude to suicide. The reason Hamlet gives for not killing himself at the start of the play is that the Christian God forbids it: 'the Everlasting had not fix'd / His canon 'gainst self-slaughter' *(Act 1, Scene 2)*. Later, in his soliloquy in Act 3, Scene 1, he is less concerned with religious beliefs and more fearful of what happens after death.

Ophelia and suicide

Ideas about suicide in Shakespeare's time also help us to explore the representation of Ophelia's death.

It is hard to be certain whether Ophelia's death is suicide. Shakespeare makes it impossible for us to be certain because:

- the audience does not see it happen. Instead Shakespeare has Gertrude report it
- the description itself is **ambiguous** (Act 4, Scene 7). It is impossible to tell from this if Ophelia intended to drown herself.

ambiguous open to more than one interpretation

Key quotations

… the dread of something after death,
The undiscover'd country
(Hamlet, Act 3, Scene 1)

As one incapable of her own distress
(Gertrude, Act 4, Scene 7)

Activity 5

'I am more an antique Roman than a Dane', says Horatio, in the final scene of the play. What idea of suicide is he referring to? What does it reveal about the character of Hamlet that he stops Horatio from drinking the poison?

Activity 6

What aspects of the beliefs about suicide outlined on pages 26-27 are referred to in the Priest's response to Laertes's question ('**What ceremony else?**') about the lack of prayers in Ophelia's burial (Act 5, Scene 1)?

Women and gender

Queen Elizabeth I ruled England during much of Shakespeare's writing career. However, during his lifetime, the majority of women had very limited rights, in legal, political and economic terms, and in their personal lives. Marriage, the production of children and the management of the household were seen as a woman's role and purpose in life.

Beliefs about women

Underpinning the beliefs about what individual women were or were not supposed to do were some fundamental beliefs about all women. Women were believed to be morally, intellectually and physically weaker than men. The Bible provided justification for this understanding, specifically in the Book of Genesis in which Eve caused the Fall of Man by disobeying God's command not to eat from the Tree of Knowledge. Religious arguments were reinforced by the classical writer Aristotle, who stated that the female body was an inferior version of the perfect male form.

Medical theories supported a strong sense of difference between men and women, which served to justify the dominance of men over women. Men were believed to be hot and dry, and women were cold and moist. It was this that supposedly made women passive, intellectually unstable and lacking in courage. (See page 60 for more information about 'humours'.)

Activity 7

Make a list of bullet points setting out the conventional ideas about women that Hamlet refers to in his first soliloquy in Act 1, Scene 2.

Women and obedience

Women were expected to obey all men in their family. Punishments for disobedience could be harsh because the religious and political authorities decreed that women existed to serve and obey men. Obedience, as Shakespeare's contemporary, the poet John Donne, wrote, 'is the cornerstone [basis] of peace'.

> **Key quotation**
>
> I shall obey, my lord.
> *(Ophelia, Act 1, Scene 3)*

Women and silence

As important as and closely connected to obedience was the virtue of silence for women. This idea also had biblical authority:

 Women should remain silent in the churches. They are not allowed to speak, but must be in submission, as the law says. If they want to inquire about something, they should ask their own husbands at home; for it is disgraceful for a woman to speak in the church.

(I Corinthians 14: 34–35)

Women and sex

Being chaste (non-sexual or innocent) was also seen as a virtue for women. In practice, a life of chastity could mean having no sex at all (the ideal in the Catholic Church and therefore the life of a nun or monk) or only having sex within marriage in order to have children (the Protestant ideal). Being unchaste was condemned, but double standards applied: a sexually active woman was much more likely to be condemned than a man.

In Shakespeare's time it was thought there was a greater need to enforce women's chastity because women were less rational than men and therefore more at the mercy of their passions and desires, or what was known as 'appetites'. This supposed inability to control themselves sexually, justified their control by men.

Key quotation

Why, she would hang on him
As if increase of appetite had grown
By what it fed on
(Hamlet, Act 1, Scene 2)

 Activity 8

In what ways is Ophelia the 'perfect woman'? Base your answers on the first three acts of *Hamlet*. For each quality you identify, provide a short quotation from the text. You could present this information in a table or a spider diagram.

Friendships between men

Bearing in mind the general belief in Shakespeare's time that women were second-class humans, it is not surprising that friendships between men were often valued more highly. Women might be needed in order to create a family, but true love and friendship was only possible between equals – between men.

Activity 9

Read through Act 5, Scene 2 from the start through to Horatio's line **'Peace, who comes here?'**

a) Explore different ways of saying the few lines that Horatio has.

b) Write a short paragraph summarizing the friendship between the two men, based on this interaction.

Activity 10

a) Who does Hamlet love more – Ophelia or Horatio?

b) How would you justify your answer to someone who didn't agree with you?

Shakespeare's sources

Shakespeare took most of the plot of *Hamlet* from a very popular, 16th-century French writer, François de Belleforest. He, in turn, had taken the Hamlet story from a chronicle (history) of the life of Amleth of Denmark, compiled in the late 12th century by a Dane known as Saxo the Grammarian.

There are two major differences between Shakespeare's *Hamlet* and his two main sources, and one striking similarity:

- In their versions, Saxo and Belleforest have a long delay, of years, before the revenge is achieved. However, this delay is not a concern, as it is in Shakespeare's play. Instead, it is a sign of the determination of the revenger.
- Shakespeare's sources end with the hero in triumph. Amleth justifies his actions to the people in a long speech, is made king and, most importantly, he is alive!

Shakespeare is similar to his sources in the representation of Gertrude and, in particular, the level of disgust expressed concerning her sexual activity. Both Saxo and Belleforest wrote long passages about the queen's repulsive, animalistic sexual appetites. Belleforest writes:

'What trust can I have in you, who, like a lascivious wanton [over-sexed woman] breaking out into every immodesty, run with outstretched arms after than villainous, treacherous tyrant who is the murderer of my father...'

(François de Belleforest, *Histories Tragiques*)

The queen is described as immodest in her behaviour, intending to attract sexual attention. The idea that immodesty is bad is central to many religions' insistence on 'modest' dress. Belleforest also makes it clear that the queen has an affair with her brother-in-law before her husband is murdered.

Shakespeare keeps much of the disgust but he doesn't make it clear whether Gertrude was Claudius's lover before Old Hamlet's death or whether she knows that Claudius is a murderer.

> **Key quotation**
>
> Lay not that flattering unction to your soul,
> That not your trespass but my madness speaks.
> It will but skin and film the ulcerous place,
> Whiles rank corruption, mining all within,
> Infects unseen.
> *(Hamlet, Act 3, Scene 4)*

Activity 11

Pretend you are a lawyer, making a case against Gertrude. Decide what her offence (**'trespass'**) actually is, using only evidence from the characters in the play. The Ghost, for example, says that Gertrude is **'seeming-virtuous'** *(Act 1, Scene 5)*. What could he mean? If Hamlet is your main witness for the prosecution, why might you have problems?

Writing about context

When showing your knowledge of context, avoid writing 'Shakespeare believes...'. For example, you may have spotted references to the divine right of kings (see page 74) in *Hamlet*, but you should remember that Shakespeare puts these ideas into the mouths of his characters. Claudius may talk about the divine right of kings in Act 4, Scene 5, but we know that there is nothing divine about the way Claudius has taken power. He is using the idea to calm Gertrude down, to impress Laertes and perhaps to reassure himself. Claudius's use of these words tells us nothing about Shakespeare's own beliefs.

Tragedy

Hamlet is described as a tragedy, which means, on the simplest level of plot, that the outcome of the play is disastrous for the **protagonist**. So *Hamlet* is a tragedy because Hamlet and other characters suffer and die.

The way people have discussed *Hamlet* over the years has been strongly influenced by the following ideas of the Greek philosopher Aristotle.

Catharsis

Aristotle (see page 19) wrote that in tragedy, the playwright creates 'incidents arousing pity and fear, wherewith to accomplish the **catharsis** of such emotions'. He is focusing on what happens to the audience when they experience tragic drama: we feel 'pity' and 'fear' but, through feeling them, we are cleansed of those emotions. Aristotle describes the paradoxical process whereby audiences feel relieved or even uplifted after a performance of a play which, logically, should have upset or depressed them.

Hamartia

This is another term from Aristotle, meaning 'error of judgement' or – as it is often described – 'tragic flaw'. It is applied to what is happening to a character on stage, rather than in the audience. In tragedy, the hero is a great man, but he is also someone who either makes a serious mistake or has one serious failing in his character. This **hamartia** leads to his downfall.

Hamlet refers to this idea when he is talking to Horatio, just before the Ghost appears to them in Act 1, Scene 4. He talks of a 'vicious mole of nature'. According to Hamlet, no one can avoid having a serious failing: it is built into them 'in their birth', so they are not guilty. However good somebody tries to be, or is, they will still 'take corruption / From that particular fault'.

> **Activity 1**
>
> What do you think is Hamlet's hamartia (Act 1, Scene 4)? To what extent does this lead to his downfall? Justify your comments with evidence from the play.

Peripeteia

Often, in a five-act tragedy, the **peripeteia** occurs in Act 3, at or near the centre point of the play. (You can see how this looks on Freytag's pyramid, in the chapter on Structure. In tragedy, the climax and peripeteia often occur at around the same time.)

Different people will see the turning point of *Hamlet* the play (or the turning point for Hamlet the character) at different moments. Some see the performance of 'The Mousetrap' in Act 3, Scene 2 as the turning point. The scene gives Hamlet what he thinks he wants, which is apparent proof of Claudius's guilt. He is then forced into action. The critic, Marjorie Garber, argues that Claudius's reaction is a crucial moment of peripeteia, for the play and for the character of Hamlet:

> From this moment, from the play's principal turning point [Act 3, Scene 2], Hamlet will himself begin to act, not only in the sense of 'perform' but also in the sense of 'do'. When he next appears, he will act, quickly and without remorse, in his mother's closet, stabbing behind the arras at the intruder he is sure is Claudius, killing Polonius instead.

An alternative moment of peripeteia could be Hamlet's final soliloquy (in Act 4, Scene 4), which is prompted by the sight of Fortinbras and his army. At this point, Hamlet at last stops thinking about things too much and/or talking to himself. He starts doing, or acting, and he starts talking to others. He also becomes a cold-blooded killer, sending Rosencrantz and Guildenstern to their deaths. In terms of setting, Hamlet is finally away from Elsinore, out in the real world, another major change. In this interpretation, it can be argued that Shakespeare separates the climax in the action ('The Mousetrap' and the revelation of Claudius's guilt) from his hero's moment of sudden change or transformation.

Activity 2

Write a paragraph either defending or disagreeing with Marjorie Garber's view of the events immediately after 'The Mousetrap', the play-within-a-play.

catharsis a Greek word meaning cleansing or purification

hamartia a tragic flaw in a character

peripeteia a sudden change in events or reversal of fortunes

protagonist the central character or leading figure in a story

What happens in tragedy?

Shakespeare did not set out to write a play that fitted Aristotle's ideas. In fact, he broke numerous 'rules' of tragedy, mixing in comic scenes, for example, and breaking the 'unities' of time, place and plot (see page 19). Aristotle's theories and terms are a useful way to think about *Hamlet* as a tragic drama, but they are not the only way to think about Shakespearean tragedy.

Tragedy can be understood in terms of what happens to members of the audience while watching. For a tragedy to be effective, they must strongly sympathize and identify with the central character. This means not simply entering into the character's feelings or mind, or feeling sorry for them, but sharing what they are going through. Members of the audience therefore experience the tragedy themselves.

Activity 3

a) Do you sympathize or identify with Hamlet or with another character in the play? Explain what makes you feel the way you do.

b) List moments in *Hamlet* that make us feel pity or fear.

Revenge tragedy

As well as Aristotle, there is another classical writer who was much more directly influential on playwrights in Shakespeare's time. This was the Roman dramatist Seneca, who wrote plays packed with murders, ghosts, violence and revenge. It appears that this is exactly what the Elizabethan audiences wanted, so playwrights produced a steady stream of 'tragedies of blood' or **revenge tragedies**, each writer trying to outdo the previous one in the portrayal of horrors on stage.

The hero in revenge tragedy

In a conventional revenge tragedy the hero has not created the situation in which he finds himself and from which the tragedy arises. Therefore hamartia or the fatal flaw is less important to the outcome. The hero does not take a fatal, misguided step, but is faced with an appalling, intolerable situation for which he has no responsibility; the time is indeed 'out of joint', as Hamlet realizes at the end of Act 1, Scene 5.

Shakespeare puts his hero Hamlet into an intolerable situation but makes this *doubly* difficult because of characteristics that would be admirable in other settings. In *Hamlet*, we see a thoughtful, witty, **melancholy** student asked to be a brutal and simplistic avenger. It is indeed an act of 'cursed spite' *(Act 1, Scene 5)*, whether by Fate or God, to give Hamlet the role of avenger.

The Spanish Tragedie:
OR,
Hieronimo is mad agains.

Containing the lamentable end of *Don Horatio*, and *Belimperia* s with the pittifull death of *Hieronimo*.

Newly corrected, amended, and enlarged with new Additions of the *Painters* part, and others, as it hath of late been divers times acted.

LONDON,
Printed by W. White, for I. White and T Langley, and are to be fold at their Shop over againft the Sarazens head without New-gate. 1615.

The Spanish Tragedy by Thomas Kyd was the first revenge play in English, written in 1587 and very popular in Shakespeare's time

melancholy sad or depressed; in Shakespeare's time, mental disturbance ranging from sadness to insanity

revenge tragedy a form of drama that is sensational and extremely violent. It was popular in Shakespeare's time and often known as 'tragedy of blood'

Activity 4

An Elizabethan book on medicine described the symptoms of melancholy as:

- feeling sad and fearful
- displaying distrust, doubt, despair
- fluctuating between fury and merriment
- use of sardonian (sardonic) and false laughter.

What evidence can you find in Hamlet's behaviour for any of these symptoms?

The plot in revenge tragedy

The plot in revenge tragedy is usually driven by the murder of a person in power or a close relative of the hero. The hero is therefore faced with the problem of how to carry out revenge against a murderer who is out of reach of ordinary justice (see page 76).

There are two important aspects to this. One is timeless: how does one bring somebody to justice who seems above the law or indeed *is* the law? The other is more specific to Shakespeare's era. *Hamlet* was written at a time when, throughout Europe, kings and queens were consolidating their power. In an attempt to stop rebellions, monarchs appealed to the idea of the divine right of kings (see pages 74 and 81). This idea makes things even harder for Hamlet. Has he got the right to kill a king, God's representative on earth?

There is one further element of the genre of revenge tragedy that is relevant to *Hamlet*. If the initial situation is not created by the hero, it must have been created by the villain. Therefore, the villain is far more important and interesting in revenge tragedy. He is often an active character, in contrast to the hero, who might be quite passive, simply responding to the actions of the villains (see the section on Claudius on page 49).

> **Key quotations**
>
> The time is out of joint. O cursed spite,
> That ever I was born to set it right. *(Hamlet, Act 1, Scene 5)*
>
> There's such divinity doth hedge a king *(Claudius, Act 4, Scene 5)*

Activity 5

Write a paragraph explaining who you think is the 'villain' in *Hamlet*, giving reasons.

Activity 6

Copy and complete the table below. All the quotations come from Act 4, Scene 5.

What Claudius says	What he means	Why is this ironic (coming from Claudius)?
'Let him go, Gertrude. Do not fear our person.'		
'There's such divinity doth hedge a king'		
'That treason can but peep to what it would, / Acts little of his will.'		

History and tragedy

Shakespeare was writing in an era when tragedy was understood in terms of history. (You can see this on the original title page, where Hamlet is designated a 'tragical history'.)

In Shakespeare's time, history meant stories of powerful people, of kings and queens. It was inconceivable to Shakespeare's contemporaries, or even perhaps to Shakespeare himself, that anyone would write a history or a tragedy with an ordinary person as the protagonist. Tragedy focused on leaders because what happened to kings, princes and emperors was significant to the whole country.

Activity 7

Write a paragraph summarizing how people who are not from the elite world are represented in *Hamlet*.

Comic elements

Comedy can be an important element in tragedy. Shakespeare often creates scenes of comedy and wit in the middle of tragedy. The most obvious comic set piece in *Hamlet* is the graveyard scene (Act 5, Scene 1). Early editions of the play include the **stage direction** 'Enter two clowns'.

Throughout the play, however, there are other moments when the audience might laugh. For example, it can be very funny when Hamlet refuses, in Act 4, Scene 3, to tell Claudius where he has put Polonius's body. Another example is the way Shakespeare has the Ghost move about under the stage in Act 1, Scene 5. Hamlet sees the funny side of it (or is he hysterical?) when he says, 'Well said, old mole', while the characters charge around the stage trying to find where the voice is coming from. Shakespeare was obviously quite comfortable mixing comedy with horror.

Shakespeare often includes comic elements within his tragedies

Writing about tragedy

When writing about tragedy, remember that there are two different ways of answering the question 'what happens in tragedy?':

- Focus on what is happening on stage, for example the suffering and deaths shown by Shakespeare, or how Shakespeare represents peripeteia or hamartia.
- Think about what happens to the audience when we watch tragedy.

Your critical understanding of the play will be helped if you can bring together your work on the play's *structure* with your work on *genre*. For example, you might have identified a climax in *Hamlet*, using the structural model of Freytag's pyramid (see page 14). Now ask yourself whether the climax can be understood in terms of the genre of tragedy. Perhaps it is a moment of peripeteia or catharsis?

Characterization and Roles

A playwright uses different methods of characterization from those used by a novelist. Novelists can provide readers with lots of background information, and can enter the minds of the characters, letting readers know what characters think, feel and are planning to do. A playwright has to use soliloquies to show a character's thoughts or have characters explaining the **back story** in dialogue (as Shakespeare does when he is setting up the Fortinbras subplot at the beginning of *Hamlet*).

Many of the stage directions you have in your edition of *Hamlet* will have been added by editors and relate mainly to physical actions. Without modern levels of stage directions, we simply do not know, for example, what clothes the characters should wear or how they should stand, look or move during a scene in which they might not speak very much.

Shakespeare uses three main techniques to create characters. They reveal themselves:

- through their own actions
- by what others say about them
- through their own language – not just *what* they say, but *how* they say it.

back story the history of what has already happened

Main characters

Hamlet

The play is dominated by the complex character of Hamlet. Two of his main characteristics are:

- his changeability: his mood can change from one moment to the next
- his inwardness: he thinks and talks a lot about what is going on in his mind.

Both these qualities give Hamlet great depth as a character but also make it very difficult to sum him up.

Hamlet as a man apart

The audience's first introduction to Hamlet, in the play's second scene, adds to the complexity. We learn more about the tensions in Hamlet's relationship with his uncle Claudius when, in Act 1, Scene 2, he ignores Claudius's long lecture about 'unmanly grief', responding to Claudius with two short sentences and to his mother Gertrude with, 'I shall in all my best obey you, madam.'

Hamlet's first soliloquy, at the end of Act 1, Scene 2, confirms what he has been thinking about. Even before he has been told about the Ghost, Hamlet reveals that he hates the world (and has therefore contemplated killing himself) and that he hates women (but is specifically disgusted by his mother's behaviour).

Activity 1

Create a series of bullet points, setting out exactly why Hamlet is so angry with his mother and with Claudius.

Activity 2

Copy and complete the table below with your first impressions of Hamlet's character. One example has been done for you.

What Hamlet says	What he means	What does this tell you about him?	What does his *way* of speaking tell you about him?
'A little more than kin, and less than kind.' *(Act 1, Scene 3)*			
'Not so, my lord, I am too much in the sun.' *(Act 1, Scene 3)*		Hamlet resents that he is now 'son' to Claudius.	

Hamlet and madness

Hamlet's sudden mood changes are visible as early as Act 1, Scene 2. He moves quickly from suicidal thoughts, to talking quite easily with Horatio, to recklessness (vowing to speak with the Ghost of his father even if **'hell itself should gape'**), to a short, closing soliloquy of restless anticipation.

However, Hamlet ends Act 1, Scene 5 in command of himself and his companions. He tells them that he will **'put an antic disposition'** on, makes them swear that they will tell no one about the Ghost, and tells the audience that **'The time is out of joint. O cursed spite, / That ever I was born to set it right.'**

The audience soon has evidence that Hamlet has indeed put on **'an antic disposition'**. In Act 2, Scene 1, Ophelia tells her father that Hamlet has burst into her closet, half-dressed, and behaving very strangely. Polonius is convinced that he has found the reason for Hamlet's madness – Ophelia's rejection of him.

Once again, Shakespeare makes it hard for the audience to make any clear judgements about Hamlet's state of mind. We see him talking nonsense and being rude to Polonius. But we also hear him give a long and apparently rational account of his depression to Rosencrantz and Guildenstern in Act 2, Scene 2. Shakespeare then repeats the same pattern. Hamlet ends his conversation with Rosencrantz and Guildenstern with some riddle-like words about madness, but immediately afterwards greets the Players warmly and rationally.

Just to confuse the audience even more, Hamlet later talks coherently and enthusiastically with the Players at the start of Act 3, Scene 2. He may be a bit patronizing (after all, he is only an amateur, lecturing professional actors on how to do their job) but he is certainly not mad, depressed or angry.

Shakespeare chooses this moment to give Hamlet a long speech, in which he tells Horatio just how much he admires him for his balanced mind.

David Tennant interprets Hamlet's state of mind, with Peter de Jersey's Horatio, in the Royal Shakespeare Company's production at The Courtyard Theatre, London, 2008

Key quotation

I am but mad north-north-west. When the wind is southerly, I know a hawk from a handsaw
(Hamlet, Act 2, Scene 2)

Activity 3

a) From what you have learned of Hamlet in Act 1, what are his three most important characteristics? Illustrate each one with a short quotation.

b) Do you think these are qualities that will enable him to 'set it right', as he says at the end of Act 1, Scene 5?

c) Turn your answers into a paragraph summarizing Shakespeare's representation of Hamlet as a revenge hero in the opening act.

Activity 4

Argue either for or against the statement that 'Hamlet is completely sane throughout Act 2, Scene 2 and only pretends to be mad when there is a strategic reason for him to do so'.

Hamlet as revenger

As Act 2, Scene 2 comes to an end, Hamlet appears to have forgotten all about the Ghost, revenge and Claudius's guilt. However, as soon as he is alone, he becomes furious with himself. He has just seen an actor, performing 'a fiction' and work himself up into an emotional state 'for nothing'. If the actor had the real 'cue for passion' that Hamlet has (the knowledge of who murdered his father), he would 'drown the stage with tears'. In contrast, Hamlet himself 'can say nothing'. Hamlet asks, 'Am I a coward?' and then answers the question himself – yes, he is. Whatever anyone would do to him, he 'should take it'.

Hamlet decides to test the truthfulness of the Ghost through the performance of a play, whilst other characters are still trying to find out the truth about Hamlet.

His soliloquy in Act 3, Scene 1 seems to take Hamlet right back to the very beginning of the play, when he wished for **'self-slaughter'** *(Act 1, Scene 2)*. Now, however, he is afraid of what happens after we die. Who, he asks, would put up with a **'weary life'**, unless he had a **'dread of something after death'** *(Act 3, Scene 1)*?

Activity 5

Copy and complete the table below. What do we learn about Hamlet and his feelings about revenge from his soliloquoy in Act 2, Scene 2?

What Hamlet says	What he means	What does this tell you about him?
'I am pigeon-liver'd and lack gall'		
'I should ha' fatted all the region kites / With this slave's offal.'		
'Remorseless, treacherous, lecherous, kindless villain!'		
'Why, what an ass am I!'		
'Prompted to my revenge by heaven and hell'		
'like a whore unpack my heart with words / And fall a-cursing like a very drab, / A scullion!'		
'About, my brains.'		

Hamlet and relationships

Shakespeare makes it hard for the audience or reader to be sure of anything about Hamlet's character, including his relationships with other characters. Immediately after the **'To be, or not to be'** soliloquy in Act 3, Scene 1, we see a vicious Hamlet verbally abusing, and in some productions physically abusing, Ophelia. Yet in Act 5, Scene 1 he says how much he loved her: **'I lov'd Ophelia. Forty thousand brothers / Could not with all their quantity of love / Make up my sum.'**

Activity 6

a) Create a series of bullet points, listing the insults that Hamlet throws at Ophelia in Act 3, Scene 1 (often referred to as 'the nunnery scene' because of Hamlet's line **'Get thee to a nunnery'**). Which of them have you heard him say before?

b) Write a short paragraph summarizing Hamlet's attitude to women in general and towards Ophelia in particular.

> **Key quotation**
>
> > Give me that man
> > That is not passion's slave, and I will wear him
> > In my heart's core, ay, in my heart of heart,
> > As I do thee.
> > *(Hamlet, Act 3, Scene 2)*

> **Activity 7**
>
> In his speech to Horatio in Act 3, Scene 2 starting **'Nay, do not think I flatter'**, Hamlet gives some examples of what he means when he talks about not being **'passion's slave'**. Write them out in your own words. Then write a paragraph to answer the following question: Do you think that Hamlet himself is **'passion's slave'**? Explain your answer.

Hamlet (Kenneth Branagh) grieves for Ophelia (Joanne Pearce) in the Royal Shakespeare Company production at the Barbican Theatre, London, 1992

Hamlet the killer

On his way to his mother, in Act 3, Scene 3, Hamlet has the perfect opportunity to kill Claudius (**'Now might I do it pat… And now I'll do it.'**) but does not. However, minutes later he does kill Polonius, mistaking him for Claudius. His reaction to becoming a killer at last is strangely calm. He spends only three lines on the dead man:

> **Key quotation**
>
> Thou wretched, rash, intruding fool, farewell.
> I took thee for thy better. Take thy fortune:
> Thou find'st to be too busy is some danger.
> *(Hamlet, Act 3, Scene 4)*

Activity 8

a) Copy the table below, which gives phrases from Hamlet's soliloquy in Act 3, Scene 3, then complete the right-hand column.

b) Complete the following sentence: Hamlet does not kill Claudius at this moment because… .

Quotation	A reason not to kill Claudius now – or a reason to kill him later?
'a goes to heaven	
'A took my father grossly	
he is fit and season'd for his passage	
in th'incestuous pleasure of his bed	
his heels may kick at heaven	

Hamlet, the son

In Hamlet's first scene (Act 1, Scene 2), it is noticeable that he responds to his mother rather than Claudius in public. In private, in the closet scene (Act 3, Scene 4), he is absolutely focused on his mother, to the extent of ignoring Polonius's dead body. It is clear therefore that Gertrude is extremely important to Hamlet, and some have interpreted his feelings for her as too strong or inappropriate.

Hamlet (Paapa Essiedu) remonstrates with Gertrude (Tanya Moodie) on her bed in this 2016 production at Stratford-upon-Avon

There is further evidence for this when he focuses on her sexual relationship with Claudius, rather than on Claudius's murder of his father. This shows that Hamlet is (at this point in the play at least) far more preoccupied with his mother's sex life than avenging his own father's death.

When Hamlet does talk about his father (in this scene and in Act 1, Scene 2), he is certain of his father's perfection. Hamlet is therefore a son who has very strong, but very different, feelings about his two parents.

Activity 9

Find some of Hamlet's words, in Act 3, Scene 4, which illustrate the following sentences:

- Gertrude does not know what Hamlet is accusing her of.
- Old Hamlet was like a god, in appearance and actions.
- Gertrude is too old to feel love/lust.
- Gertrude cannot see the Ghost.
- Gertrude believes that Hamlet is mad.
- Hamlet is not mad.
- Gertrude should not have sex with Claudius.

Hamlet's delay

It is difficult to know why Hamlet delays revenging the murder of his father. Hamlet himself says he simply does 'not know / Why yet I live to say this thing's to do' *(Act 4, Scene 4)*. In Act 1, Scene 5, Hamlet says that he would 'sweep' to his revenge, with 'wings as swift / As meditation', but this seems harder to do that than he thought.

The question of why Hamlet delays is very important to our experience of watching *Hamlet* and the answer can be approached in different ways:

- by focusing on Hamlet's character: for example, he is too thoughtful to act in any way at all
- by focusing on the political situation: Hamlet delays because, whatever the provocation, no one has the right to kill a king
- by questioning the status of the Ghost, which might be a devil in disguise. This lies behind Hamlet's determination (expressed at the end of Act 2, Scene 2) to 'have these players / Play something like the murder of my father / Before mine uncle'. If Claudius 'do blench' (flinches), Hamlet will know what to do. The alternative, as he explains to Horatio in Act 3, Scene 2, is that if Claudius does not reveal his guilt, then 'It is a damned ghost that we have seen, / And my imaginations are as foul / As Vulcan's stithy.'

Once he is back in Denmark, having dispatched Rosencrantz and Guildenstern to their fate, it is even more difficult to understand why Hamlet delays. He has already become a killer, first in the heat of the moment (and getting the wrong man), but then cold-bloodedly sending Rosencrantz and Guildenstern to their deaths.

The question of why Hamlet is able to act at the end of the play is related to the question of why he delays, and Shakespeare brings the two together in Hamlet's final soliloquy. Hamlet watches, in shame, as twenty thousand men march to their 'imminent death' for 'a fantasy' in Act 4, Scene 4. They will be fighting for a piece of land that is not even big enough to bury their bodies.

Activity 10

In his final soliloquy in Act 4, Scene 4, Hamlet considers his **'dull revenge'**, concluding with **'O, from this time forth / My thoughts be bloody or be nothing worth.'**

Try to identify other moments in the play when Hamlet has expressed similar feelings. Is there any reason to believe that he means what he says now?

Violent Hamlet

When we next see Hamlet in Act 5, Scene 1, he fights with Laertes, claiming that he has **'something dangerous'** within him. There have already been indications of this harsher, more 'bloody' side to Hamlet and the language of blood runs through the play (see the section on Repetition on page 59).

In Act 3, Scene 4, Hamlet looks forward to turning the tables on Rosencrantz and Guildenstern (**'tis the sport to have the enginer / Hoist with his own petard**), and to the moment he will **'blow them at the moon'**. He also shows no respect for the dead Polonius: **'I'll lug the guts into the neighbour room.'**

However, in Act 5, Hamlet appears much calmer. It seems he has reached a new understanding both of his position (as potential revenger) and his place in the world.

Activity 11

a) Copy and complete the table below, which contains some of Hamlet's lines from the final scene of the play *(Act 5, Scene 2).*

b) Then write a paragraph exploring how Hamlet's character has changed.

What Hamlet says	Why is the line important?	How has he changed?
There's a divinity that shapes our ends, / Rough-hew them how we will –		
Why, even in that was heaven ordinant. / I had my father's signet in my purse		
is't not perfect conscience / To quit him with this arm?		
There is a special providence in the fall of a sparrow.		
The readiness is all. Since no man, of aught he leaves, knows aught, what is't to leave betimes? Let be.		

Conclusions about Hamlet's character

It remains hard to answer the question: Why is Hamlet able to take action at the end of the play? On the one hand, he has become more violent and passionate. On the other hand, he has become more passive and fatalistic.

Perhaps the two ideas can be brought together. Hamlet now sees himself as an instrument of God: **'there's a divinity that shapes our ends'** ('ends' meaning both our goals and our deaths). At the same time, he believes that **'the readiness is all'** and that the only way he can fulfil divine providence is to **'Let be'** *(Act 5, Scene 2)*.

If you are struggling to come to any firm conclusions about the character of Hamlet, bear in mind that the other characters also struggle. In the play, Claudius, motivated by fear, spends a lot of time trying to interpret Hamlet's words and actions. At least five other characters are also asked or commanded by Claudius to interpret Hamlet's behaviour (Polonius, Ophelia, Gertrude, Rosencrantz and Guildenstern). In the face of this, it is not surprising that Hamlet is keen to hide the truth (about the Ghost but also about himself) from the other characters. He therefore keeps everyone, including the audience, guessing.

There are, however, two moments at the very end of the play when characters sum up Hamlet's life and character:

- Horatio says: **'Now cracks a noble heart. Good night, sweet prince, / And flights of angels sing thee to thy rest.'**
- Fortinbras asks for Hamlet's body to be displayed like a soldier: **'For he was likely, had he been put on, / To have prov'd most royal'**.

Hamlet's own final words are fittingly **enigmatic**: **'the rest is silence'**.

Shakespeare makes the audience question what it is to be a hero and, specifically, what it is to be an avenging hero. So much has been said in the play, by so many people, and so few of the **'Words, words, words'** *(Act 2, Scene 2)* have done any good. Just as he wished in Act 1, Scene 5 that the perturbed spirit of his father could **'rest'**, Hamlet can now rest in peace, in the sleep of death.

> **enigmatic** difficult to understand, mysterious

Activity 12

Which of the two assessments of Hamlet's character, by Horatio or Fortinbras, do you think is the more accurate? Do they both have some truth in them? Explain your answer with close reference to the text.

Polonius

Polonius is the father of Laertes and Ophelia, and Claudius's loyal right-hand man, used by the king in his increasingly desperate efforts to get Hamlet under control. As a father, he represents patriarchal authority. Thinking about him in terms of the political set-up in the play, Polonius is a perfect example of the trusted advisor, a role seen as important to the proper working of monarchy in Shakespeare's time.

In Polonius's first two scenes, in the court and with his children, he comes across as long-winded and pompous, both in public and private. However, in the midst of his long, wordy speeches there is some good advice.

> **Key quotation**
>
> Neither a borrower nor a lender be,
> For loan oft loses both itself and friend [...]
> This above all: to thine own self be true,
> And it must follow as the night the day
> Thou canst not then be false to any man.
> *(Polonius, Act 1, Scene 3)*

Polonius is in a number of comic scenes. He is usually the person we (and Hamlet and everyone else on stage) are laughing at. There is even a touch of humour in the way that Polonius is killed, not least because Hamlet has got the wrong man. And the aftermath of his death has some darkly comic moments, as Polonius, reduced to 'guts' in Act 3, Scene 4, becomes part of Hamlet's game of hide and seek in Act 4, Scene 3.

David Calder as Polonius, with Rory Kinnear's Hamlet, in a performance at the Olivier Theatre, London in 2010

However, Hamlet's view of Polonius as a 'foolish prating knave' (in the closet scene in Act 3, Scene 4), and his apparent complete lack of remorse at his killing, is only one view of the character.

Activity 13

Copy and complete the table below. Find evidence for each of these characteristics in the character of Polonius. Use evidence from his actions and what he says.

Characteristic	Evidence from what Polonius does	Evidence from what Polonius says
Well-meaning, loving father		
Giver of good advice		
Willing to be laughed at		
Unintentionally comic		
Trusted political advisor		
Overbearing bully		
Insensitive to others		
Admits he's wrong		

Activity 14

Hamlet says, **'Thou wretched, rash, intruding fool, farewell'** in Act 3, Scene 4. Explain how and why Hamlet may have misjudged Polonius.

Horatio

Horatio is Hamlet's closest friend and the only person Hamlet trusts. Like Hamlet, he was a student at Wittenburg University but has come to Elsinore for Old Hamlet's funeral. Crucially, he is *not* **'passion's slave'** *(Act 3, Scene 2)*: this is why Hamlet admires and loves him (see Activity 7 on page 42). Horatio's rationality means that, in the first scene of the play, the guards invite him to come and witness the Ghost with his own eyes and speak to it.

Horatio is a minor character in terms of his number of lines and Shakespeare does not develop his character during the course of the play. However, this stability is part of Horatio's appeal. It is no coincidence that Hamlet turns to Horatio at the end of the play, in Act 5, Scene 2, to **'Report me and my cause aright / To the unsatisfied'**, and tell Hamlet's story. And it is Horatio who not only provides a summary of the play, but also says the final, extremely moving, **'Good night'** to Hamlet.

Key quotation

**Now cracks a noble heart. Good night, sweet prince,
And flights of angels sing thee to thy rest.**
(Act 5, Scene 2)

Activity 15

Contrast Hamlet's friendship with Horatio with his relationship with Ophelia. Explore not just how the characters feel about each other, but how they behave in each other's company.

Claudius

Claudius is the brother of the recently dead King Hamlet. He is therefore young Hamlet's uncle. At the start of the play we learn that he has just married Gertrude, Old Hamlet's wife (and young Hamlet's mother). Claudius asks Hamlet to think of him as a father, just two months after the death of his real father.

The newly crowned King Claudius begins the play in complete command of a big public scene in Act 1, Scene 2. He is obviously a powerful man, a good public speaker and very capable of dealing with people and politics. He manages to move effortlessly from expressing sorrow at the death of his brother to celebrating his own swift marriage to the same brother's wife: **'Therefore our sometime sister, now our queen'**.

This smooth operator is, of course, the villain of the play. Many productions of *Hamlet* portray Claudius to be a capable, strong and charming king, appearing genuine in his desire to be a good father to Hamlet (**'Our chiefest courtier, cousin, and our son'**) in Act 1, Scene 2, utterly in love with Gertrude, and quick to deal with the political and military threat from Norway.

It is important to the tension of the play that the audience doesn't know for sure that Claudius has indeed murdered his brother until he himself hints at it in an **aside** in Act 3, Scene 1 and then admits it in his soliloquy in Act 3, Scene 3. Up to that moment, all we have to show his guilt is the word of a ghost (who may be a devil) and the evidence that the unstable, grieving Hamlet hates him, primarily because of Claudius's marriage to his mother.

As the play progresses, Claudius's problems increase. Typically, he sets out the challenges he faces to his **'dear Gertrude'** in a clear way, immediately after having sent Horatio to keep a **'good watch'** on the mad Ophelia, in Act 4, Scene 5.

aside a kind of stage whisper, a behind-the-hand comment made to the audience, that other characters cannot hear

Activity 16

Mark up a copy of Claudius's speech in Act 4, Scene 5 (beginning, **'O, this is the poison of deep grief...'**), highlighting:

- the threats to Claudius's power
- where you think Claudius is telling the truth
- where he is mixing truth with lies.

Activity 17

Find evidence and a short quotation to illustrate each of the following aspects of Claudius's character. Colour-code the qualities that you think are admirable and those which are not. (You may need both colours in some cases!)

- Clever/shrewd
- Uses others to do his dirty work
- Calm in a crisis
- Loves Gertrude
- Ruthless

- Unable to repent
- Fears Hamlet
- A politician, not a soldier
- Persuasive

Laertes

Laertes is the son of Polonius and the brother of Ophelia. He is a straightforward character, at least in comparison to Hamlet. We only meet him briefly in the opening scenes, when he is permitted to leave Denmark and then says goodbye to his sister, when he warns her not to put too much trust in Hamlet. Laertes becomes much more important as a character and to the play when he returns to Elsinore, having heard of his father's murder. He is absolutely focused on revenge, but he is also all too easy for Claudius to manipulate.

Laertes has a single moment of doubt in the final scene, but – in yet more evidence of his single-minded approach, which was broken earlier only for a few seconds by his tears for Ophelia – he stays focused on revenge. He can therefore be seen as an alternative revenge hero, contrasting sharply with Hamlet, who delays and debates the issue.

Key quotation

To hell, allegiance! Vows to the blackest devil!
Conscience and grace to the profoundest pit!
I dare damnation. To this point I stand,
That both the worlds I give to negligence,
Let come what comes, only I'll be reveng'd
Most throughly for my father.
(Laertes, Act 4, Scene 5)

Activity 18

Write three short paragraphs about how the play represents Laertes's quest for vengeance.

a) The first should examine the moments when you admire Laertes.

b) The second should examine the moments when you feel critical of him.

c) Then write a final short paragraph considering Laertes's death. Does the manner of his dying confirm or change your view of his character?

Gertrude

Gertrude is the mother of Hamlet, and – more problematically – the 'sometime sister' (as Claudius describes her in Act 1, Scene 2), now wife and queen, of King Claudius. She has married Claudius very quickly after the death of her first husband, Hamlet's father. Perhaps Shakespeare is encouraging the audience to question Gertrude's love and loyalty to Old Hamlet, since she moves on so swiftly to his brother. (You will find some interesting material about Shakespeare's sources for the character of Gertrude on page 31.)

Gertrude played by Imogen Stubbs, with Ben Wishaw's Hamlet, in the 2005 production at the Old Vic Theatre, London

Although Gertrude is often present on stage, she does not say many lines. Throughout the play, she shows apparent obedience to, and acceptance of the views of, the men in her life. 'I shall obey you', she says to Claudius, for example, just before he and Polonius spy on her son Hamlet in the nunnery scene (Act 3, Scene 1). When Hamlet confronts her in the closet scene (Act 3, Scene 4), she quickly crumbles under his onslaught, saying that his words are like 'daggers' that 'cleft my heart in twain'.

Some therefore see Gertrude as a weak, passive character, someone who does not want to confront unpleasant realities. However, there are a number of small occasions where the queen does assert herself. She appears to correct Claudius when he muddles up the names of Rosencrantz and Guildenstern; she tries to get Polonius to get to the point ('More matter with less art') in Act 2, Scene 2; and, when watching the Player queen promise never to marry again if she becomes a widow, Gertrude comments that 'The lady doth protest too much, methinks' (Act 3, Scene 2).

The **tragic irony** in Gertrude's death is that it happens because she disobeys Claudius in the final scene of the play. When he says 'Gertrude, do not drink', she replies, 'I will, my lord, I pray you pardon me.'

There are only two female characters in *Hamlet* and Shakespeare makes sure that they are connected in our mind. One of Gertrude's most important moments on stage, and certainly one of her longest and most poetic speeches, comes when she describes Ophelia's death. Similarly, Gertrude is given beautiful, gentle lines to say over Ophelia's grave in sharp contrast to the violent posturing from Laertes and then Hamlet in the same scene.

> **tragic irony** when the audience knows more than the character and there is a tragic outcome

Activity 19

Annotate a copy of Act 1, Scene 2, from the beginning of Gertrude's speech, **'Good Hamlet, cast thy nighted colour off…'** to the beginning of Hamlet's soliloquy. Show what this section reveals about:

a) Gertrude   **b)** Claudius   **c)** Hamlet.

Activity 20

What do you learn about Gertrude *and* Ophelia from the following lines?

[Scattering flowers] **Sweets to the sweet. Farewell.**
I hop'd thou shouldst have been my Hamlet's wife:
I thought thy bride-bed to have deck'd, sweet maid,
And not have strew'd thy grave.
(Gertrude, Act 5, Scene 1)

Tips for assessment

When writing about Gertrude, you can strengthen your textual analysis by commenting on whether her representation reflects and/or challenges ideas about women in general in Shakespeare's time. For example:

- Gertrude's relatively small number of lines in the play might indicate that she is an unimportant character. However, in Shakespeare's time, the ideal for a woman would have been silence, therefore her lack of words could suggest that she is to be admired.

- We might see Hamlet's extreme horror at his mother's sexual activity as a sign of his own sick mind. But, in Shakespeare's time, it was conventional to attack women for being unable to control their own desires. In this light, Hamlet's disgust, although intense, might be seen as less extreme.

Ophelia

Ophelia is the daughter of Polonius and sister to Laertes. Prince Hamlet has been, and perhaps still is, in love with her.

Ophelia is characterized, for the first three acts of the play, by her obedience and passivity. A typical line is, **'I think nothing, my lord'**, spoken in the play-within-a-play scene in Act 3, Scene 2. She is told what to think (for example, about Prince Hamlet's love) and, like a good daughter, does what she is told, including rejecting Hamlet and then lying to him. On more than one occasion, she has to endure cruel treatment from Hamlet, first in Act 3, Scene 1 and then in the play-within-a-play.

There are glimpses not only of intelligence and **eloquence** in Ophelia, but even an occasional feistiness, but they are rare. She speaks beautifully about Hamlet's madness in Act 3, Scene 1 and, earlier, in Act 1, Scene 3, she tells her brother not to lecture her on being good, when he himself has no intention of being so. Laertes, she points out, has told her to follow 'the steep and thorny way to heaven', but, she fears, he will not follow his own advice and will instead follow 'the primrose path of dalliance' *(Act 1, Scene 3)*.

Everything changes in Act 4. Ophelia appears on stage out of her wits, singing snatches of songs and, in her second appearance, handing out flowers (perhaps imaginary). (You can read more about these flowers on page 63.)

Ophelia's songs would have been shocking to the audience in Shakespeare's time in a variety of ways. Although Shakespeare often adds music into his plays, it is usually performed or led by a character who is expected, or paid, to make music, including the fool Feste in *Twelfth Night* or Balthazar, the servant/musician in *Much Ado About Nothing*. The musical performances would therefore be of a high standard. Ophelia's case is different: she is not a professional musician and she sings songs, on her own, that are amateur, raw and reveal her madness and desperation rather than entertain.

What makes the scene even more shocking is that the music would be familiar to the audience in Shakespeare's time, since Ophelia sings popular songs when almost the only other music in *Hamlet* is that of the court (for example, fanfares from trumpets) or of war (more trumpets).

Those who see Ophelia in her state of madness are understandably upset and full of pity. At the same time, they are fearful. Horatio uses the word 'dangerous' in Act 4, Scene 5 and later in the same scene the king commands that a watch be kept on her. Ophelia's madness may be personally tragic for her, but it is part of a bigger political crisis unfolding in the play.

> **eloquence** the ability to use language well and persuasively

---

Key quotation

Young men will do't if they come to't –
By Cock, they are to blame.
Quoth she, 'Before you tumbled me,
You promis'd me to wed.'
(Ophelia, Act 4, Scene 5)

 Activity 21

Read out loud the dialogue between Hamlet and Ophelia in Act 3, Scene 2. How does it feel to speak Ophelia's lines? What does this suggest to you about Ophelia's character in the play?

Minor characters

Old Hamlet/the Ghost

The Ghost is the former King of Denmark, Hamlet's father, and Claudius's brother.

The character dominates the opening act of *Hamlet*, setting in motion the revenge plot with the revelation that he was murdered by Claudius. There are three ways of thinking about the Ghost, all of which are explored in the play:

- Old Hamlet might be an 'honest ghost', as Hamlet describes him in Act 1, Scene 5.
- The ghost 'May be a devil', as Hamlet worries at the end of Act 2, Scene 2, and may not be telling the truth.
- The Ghost might be a product of Hamlet's imagination, something both Hamlet and his mother believe at times.

Activity 22

What evidence can you find to argue against Gertrude's comment below about the Ghost?

This is the very coinage of your brain.
This bodiless creation ecstasy
Is very cunning in.
(Gertrude, Act 3, Scene 4)

Fortinbras

Fortinbras is the nephew of the King of Norway. Before the play begins, we learn that his father lost his life and lands in single combat with Old Hamlet.

Fortinbras is described at the beginning of the play. Horatio calls him 'young Fortinbras', who is of 'unimproved mettle, hot and full' *(Act 1, Scene 1)*. Then in Act 1, Scene 2 Claudius speaks of young Fortinbras, who has spotted an opportunity, in the death of Old Hamlet, to demand the surrender of the lands lost by his father to Old Hamlet. This sums up the young leader: he is hotheaded, full of energy and, as Claudius says, looking to exploit the apparent political instability in Denmark.

Shakespeare does not develop the character of Fortinbras and he is more talked about than present in the play. However, he appears with his army in Act 4, Scene 4 and then at the end of the play, becoming the new King of Denmark. When Fortinbras looks at the dead bodies in Elsinore he sees a political tragedy and a political opportunity.

Activity 23

Some productions cut Fortinbras out entirely or minimize his role in the final scene. Why do you think Shakespeare includes him in the play?

Rosencrantz and Guildenstern

These two characters are summoned to Elsinore from Wittenburg where they have been studying with Hamlet. They are apparently his friends, but Claudius hopes to use them to find out the reason for Hamlet's wild and threatening behaviour. Hamlet is extremely wary of his former schoolfellows. By the time he speaks with his mother in the closet scene in Act 3, Scene 4, he says he will trust them as 'adders fang'd' (in other words, not at all). They are, when it comes down to it, just another pair of spies in a play concerned with spying.

The fact that Gertrude has to remind Claudius which man is which suggests that Shakespeare has made these two characters almost interchangeable. Both are obedient to Claudius, and both attempt to be charming and friendly to Hamlet, on the surface at least.

The off stage killings of Rosencrantz and Guildenstern might, ironically, be their most significant moment, since it reveals so much about Hamlet. He is now a man who can, at the start of Act 5, Scene 2, dismiss their deaths as 'not near my conscience' because they brought the violence upon themselves.

> **Key quotation**
>
> Horatio: So Guildenstern and Rosencrantz go to't.
> Hamlet: Why, man, they did make love to this employment.
>   They are not near my conscience
>
> *(Act 5, Scene 2)*

Tips for assessment

When writing about minor characters, it is useful to consider not only the character in question, but also his/her significance in relation to the main characters.

Osric

The courtier Osric, who appears in Act 5, Scene 2 to tell Hamlet that Claudius asks him to engage in a fencing match with Laertes, is superficial and sycophantic (using flattery and behaving insincerely in order to get a reward or popularity). Hamlet and Horatio mock him to his face, and once he has gone Hamlet sums him up memorably – he **'did comply with his dug before 'a sucked it'** (that is, he paid formal compliments to his mother's nipple before he fed from it).

Osric can be seen to represent the court at its worst, not only in his style (although that is **satirized**) but possibly also in the way apparent politeness covers up the diseased world beneath.

> **satirize** ridicule, condemn

The two gravediggers (or clowns)

The Gravedigger and his companion are two of the few non-royal, or non-courtly, characters who appear for any length of time in the play. For a brief time, their views are heard, particularly with regard to the special treatment that Ophelia is getting as a gentlewoman: **'Will you ha' the truth an't? If this had not been a gentlewoman, she should have been buried out o' Christian burial'** *(Act 5, Scene 1).*

Samuel West's Hamlet in conversation with the gravediggers (Alan David and Conor Moloney) at Stratford-upon-Avon in 2001

As with Rosencrantz and Guildenstern, the Gravedigger gives insight into Hamlet's character. In particular, the graveyard scene provides an opportunity to hear about Hamlet's childhood.

In the graveyard scene, Hamlet not only encounters death physically, in the form of Yorick's skull, but also has conversations about death and mortality with the Gravedigger. The dialogue between prince and labourer can be seen as crucial to Hamlet's development, taking him in a new direction, far removed from the abstract musings in his earlier soliloquies (such as the famous **'To be, or not to be…'** speech in Act 3, Scene 1).

Activity 24

What ideas do the gravediggers present about death and mortality? Find quotations for each.

The Players

The Players have a crucial part in the plot, being used by Hamlet to prove Claudius's guilt. They can also have a function similar to the gravediggers in that they reveal, at least indirectly, what Hamlet was like before his father died, showing that then he was a man who thoroughly enjoyed the theatre. Indeed, for a moment in Act 2, Scene 2, when he welcomes them, it seems that the old Hamlet is back and he happily gets caught up in his pleasure in all things theatrical.

Activity 25

Describe the events before and during the performance of 'The Mousetrap' from the point of view of the Players. For example, your first point could be that they arrive in Elsinore and are greeted by Prince Hamlet.

The soldiers Marcellus, Francisco and Barnardo

These minor characters are interchangeable and not developed in any way, but they are significant to the play as a whole in two ways. They are important because they are the first characters we meet, in Act 1, Scene 1, and their words and actions set the atmosphere for the play – fear and uncertainty, disease and darkness.

> **Key quotation**
>
> 'Tis bitter cold,
> And I am sick at heart.
> *(Francisco, Act 1, Scene 1)*

Later in the scene, they ask Horatio, anxiously, about the preparations for war.

These soldiers are also significant because all three see the Ghost (unlike Gertrude later), suggesting that the Ghost is not simply a figment of Hamlet's imagination.

Writing about characters

- Always try to write about a character's role or function in the play as a whole. For example, Hamlet is usually viewed as the tragic hero, with Ophelia as a victim of tragedy.

- Always try to show how the character might change across the course of the play or make it clear that the character does not change.

- Try to be alert to the different ways in which a character is seen by other characters.

Language

Shakespeare uses many different kinds of language in *Hamlet*. Sometimes his characters speak in extremely structured, formal language and at other times in very colloquial language. As the critic Frank Kermode writes, in *Hamlet* there is a 'constantly shifting **register** not only of action but of language'; there is 'limitless variation'.

> **register** the form of a language used by a social group or in a particular social setting (e.g. slang)

Soliloquies

A soliloquy is a speech spoken by a character alone on stage. Shakespeare uses soliloquies to reveal the true, hidden feelings and thoughts of his characters. In the world of Elsinore, there are many secrets, so these moments are even more important. Hamlet's seven soliloquies are the most important in the play. They occur when Hamlet is in intense emotional or psychological crisis, showing him either distressed or confused, or trying to work out something in his mind or feelings. If you track the soliloquies, they show Hamlet's psychological journey – and reveal that it is far from straightforward.

Claudius's soliloquy in Act 3, Scene 3 is significant in a different way because it reveals not only that he is definitely a murderer, but also his unwillingness to give up what he's gained from killing and his inability to pray. Claudius's second, shorter soliloquy in Act 4, Scene 3 is another example of dramatic irony, when he reveals to the audience his plan for the 'present death of Hamlet'.

Usually, only the most important characters in a play have soliloquies. They increase the character's depth and help the audience to feel a closer connection with the character. Shakespeare was writing in a time when it was generally believed that men were more rational and capable of thought than women, and when men held more power. Therefore, it is unsurprising that most of Shakespeare's soliloquies are given to male characters, because they are more likely to be the characters with the attributes of power and eloquence.

Shakespeare appears to give Ophelia a short soliloquy, when Hamlet leaves her with the command, 'To a nunnery, go', in Act 3, Scene 1. However, it can be argued that she is not truly alone on stage, because her father and her king are still eavesdropping, even if they do not enter until she has finished her speech.

Soliloquies can be related to an aside, in which a character makes a brief comment to the audience. The dramatic convention is that the other characters on stage cannot hear what they say. An aside is a useful way for a playwright to give the audience hints concerning plot or character.

Activity 1

'Ophelia's soliloquy in Act 3, Scene 1 reveals nothing about her own character, but is completely focused on Hamlet.' Write a couple of paragraphs arguing for or against this statement.

Activity 2

Find an example of an aside from the play and describe its effect on the audience.

Repetition

In Shakespeare's time, the action of *Hamlet* unfolded on a relatively bare stage, in daylight, with almost no stage machinery. Shakespeare therefore had to create a sense of setting or time through language, rather than scenery and lighting. On one level, therefore, Shakespeare's use of language is entirely functional: when a character says 'Good night', for example, it helps us know where we are in the timeline of the play. In the opening scene, the phrase is used in this way, to show that it is night.

But, through repetition, the words gain more significance over the course of the play. There is a whole cluster of 'Good nights' in the middle of the play. Ophelia, in her madness, says 'Good night' repeatedly, adding to the pathos of her madness. Hamlet says the phrase no less than five times to his mother in the closet scene, far more than is actually needed in the circumstances. His repetition makes him sound almost crazed, despite the fact that he claims he is completely sane. There is one last use of 'Good night' in the play, at the very end.

> **Key quotation**
>
> Come, my coach. Good night, ladies, good night. Sweet ladies, good night, good night. *(Ophelia, Act 4, Scene 5)*

Activity 3

Find the final occurrence of 'Good night' in the play. What makes this particular one so moving? (Note that the sentence contains another word which occurs many times through the play: 'rest'.)

Another simple word, 'blood', appears throughout the play and with good reason. Revenge tragedies are also known as 'tragedies of blood'. This is a reference not just to the level of violence in the plays, but also to the underlying reasons for the violence.

In Shakespeare's time, a person's physical and psychological characteristics were thought to be determined by a combination of fluids, or humours, within the body. There were four humours but the two most relevant to *Hamlet* are melancholy (also called black bile) and blood. In a healthy, sane person, the four humours were in balance and properly blended. Medical books argued that if one of the humours was out of balance, the person might become ill.

> **Key quotation**
>
> O, from this time forth / My thoughts be bloody, or be nothing worth.
> *(Hamlet, Act 4, Scene 4)*

Activity 4

Complete a copy of the table below, including quotations when Hamlet uses the word 'blood'. Suggest the meaning for each quotation in your own words. One has been done for you.

Quotation	What it means
'a fashion and a toy in blood' *(Laertes, Act 1, Scene 3)*	
'When the blood burns, how prodigal the soul / Lends the tongue vows' *(Polonius, Act 1, Scene 3)*	
'blest are those / Whose blood and judgment are so well commeddled / That they are not a pipe for Fortune's finger / To sound what stop she please' *(Hamlet, Act 3, Scene 2)*	Hamlet admires Horatio because he sees the balance of humours in him. It is this that allows Horatio to not be 'passion's slave', because his blood is balanced with judgement.
'Now could I drink hot blood' *(Hamlet, Act 3, Scene 2)*	
'How stand I then, / That have a father kill'd, a mother stain'd, / Excitements of my reason and my blood, / And let all sleep' *(Hamlet, Act 4, Scene 4)*	

Activity 5

If you search for occurrences of the word 'blood', you will see that, even though Hamlet says in Act 4, Scene 4 that his thoughts will be **'bloody, or be nothing worth'**, he does not use the word for the rest of the play. Who uses it most in the final scenes? What might be the significance of this?

Imagery

Shakespeare uses **imagery** and clusters of images in each of his plays. In *Hamlet* these image clusters often centre on disease, death and corruption.

When the natural world is referred to, it is often seen as corrupted in some way. Corruption can be thought of in different ways, including our modern understanding of political corruption, but the word also has older meanings, which include ideas of sin and decay. In Hamlet's first soliloquy in Act 1, Scene 2, for example, he describes the world as an 'unweeded garden / That grows to seed'.

Specific reference to a corrupt garden would have been doubly powerful to an audience in Shakespeare's time, because they believed the story of the first humans, Adam and Eve, as told in the Book of Genesis in the Bible. Although strictly forbidden by God to do so, Eve ate the fruit from the Tree of Knowledge in the Garden of Eden. She was tempted by the Devil in the form of a serpent. Eve's disobedience led to Adam and Eve being forced to leave the Garden of Eden, punished by God with suffering and death.

Adam and Eve in the Garden of Eden

Later, Claudius makes another **allusion** to the Book of Genesis, in Act 3, Scene 3. He calls the murder of his brother an act with 'the primal eldest curse' upon it. He is referring to the biblical story in which Cain kills his brother Abel (Genesis 4: 11–12), becoming the first murderer. (Cain and Abel were the sons of Adam and Eve.)

Dust is another image that runs through the play, also alluding to the Bible:

 By the sweat of your brow you will eat your food until you return to the ground, since from it you were taken: for dust you are and to dust you will return.

(Genesis 3: 19)

allusion reference

imagery figurative (non-literal) language, especially metaphors and similes

Activity 6

Find five **metaphors** or **similes** in the play that refer to disease.

Tips for assessment

In your writing, it is good to identify and explain any allusions to the Bible where they are relevant. Linking your comments to a reading of the play is even better. Why, for example, might it be significant that Hamlet makes many more references to the Bible in the final act?

metaphor when a person or thing is described by comparison with someone or something else without using words such as 'like' or 'as', e.g. 'you are a rock'

simile when a person or thing is described by comparison with someone or something else, using words such as 'like' or 'as', e.g. 'you are like a rock'

Classical references

Shakespeare's audiences were not only very familiar with the Bible, but also with classical myths, legends and history. Copies of classical texts were available during Shakespeare's time, both in the original Latin and in English translation, and classical works made up the bulk of reading in schools.

Hamlet compares his father to Hyperion, Jove, Mars and Mercury in Act 3, Scene 4, whilst the graveyard scene (Act 5, Scene 1) has references to figures from ancient history, such as Alexander the Great and Julius Caesar. Hamlet's reference to Alexander, king of the ancient Greek kingdom of Macedonia and the greatest conqueror known to the classical world, in relation to death is not original. It was often noted that death comes to everyone, including the most powerful, such as Alexander.

Julius Caesar, the Roman general who became dictator of the Roman Republic, was often mentioned in conjunction with Alexander.

In Act 1, Scene 2, Hamlet compares himself to Hercules, a classical hero known for his great strength and courage, and for his performance of twelve labours. Hamlet sees his father as this kind of hero, but sees himself as the complete opposite. Here, a classical reference not only shows us what Hamlet is not, but also reveals that he does know himself.

Hamlet compares himself unfavourably to the classical hero, Hercules, known for his strength and courage

Symbolism

There are many examples of Shakespeare's use of **symbolism** in *Hamlet*.

The language of flowers

In the scene of her madness, Ophelia hands out flowers and sprigs of plants to the other characters, giving each of them symbolic significance: 'There's rosemary, that's for remembrance [...] There's rue for you [...] We may call it herb of grace a Sundays' *(Act 4, Scene 5)*.

Shakespeare continues to link Ophelia with flowers both in the description of her death and then at her burial. This might show her connection with the beauty of the natural world. However, the link between Ophelia and these plants is perhaps not as innocent as it might seem, even in the mad scene. Rue, for example, was used in Shakespeare's time to bring on abortions. Is it significant that Ophelia hands out flowers and sprigs from particular plants?

The language of flowers was also closely connected with women's chastity. A woman who loses her virginity was described as 'deflowered'. When Ophelia first appears, in Act 1, Scene 3, her brother insists that she should 'fear' sex (deflowering) because it is like a 'canker' worm invading and injuring a delicate flower before its buds, or 'buttons', have had time to open.

> **symbolism** the use of concrete objects in language to represent abstract ideas or concepts

---

Key quotation

Therewith fantastic garlands did she make
Of crow-flowers, nettles, daisies, and long purples,
That liberal shepherds give a grosser name
(Gertrude, Act 4, Scene 7)

Activity 7

Read Ophelia's lines in her second appearance, in Act 4 Scene 5, and note the flowers she refers to. Then complete a table like the one below.

Name of the flower	What it represents symbolically	To whom might Ophelia give it – and why?

Activity 8

Read the account of Ophelia's death in Act 4, Scene 7 and burial in Act 5, Scene 1, and make a note of when and why flowers are mentioned. Use these notes, with your table from Activity 7, to comment on what Shakespeare's use of flower imagery and symbolism suggests about Ophelia.

Death and mortality

Hamlet is full of the imagery of death, but there is only one obvious symbol of death in the play – the skull. The Gravedigger finds the skull of Yorick, the court jester Hamlet knew and loved as a young boy. Most productions show Hamlet actually touching the skull, confronting the physical reality of death.

Hamlet's encounter with Yorick's skull can be seen as a turning point (peripetaia) for him. He goes on to consider what happens to everyone's body, including that of Alexander the Great, and concludes that death is indeed the great leveller. This realization is relevant to ideas at the time the play was written about tragedy, history and politics, as expressed by writers such as Philip Sidney (see page 82).

> **Key quotations**
>
> **Alas, poor Yorick. I knew him, Horatio**
> *(Hamlet, Act 5, Scene 1)*
>
> **Alexander died, Alexander was buried, Alexander returneth to dust, the dust is earth**
> *(Hamlet, Act 5, Scene 1)*

Ophelia's language

In Shakespeare's time women were expected to be silent, chaste and obedient (see page 28). This means that when Hamlet abuses Ophelia in Act 3, Scene 1 (he tells her that, if she marries, she will be a 'breeder of sinners', and to go to a 'nunnery', which could mean a religious house or a brothel), Ophelia simply has to take the abuse in silence. If she was to respond, it would show that she knows what he is talking about. Exactly the same thing happens in the play-within-a-play scene in Act 3, Scene 2, when jokes about 'country matters' and lying 'between maids' legs' are met by Ophelia with polite silence.

However, in her madness, Ophelia speaks a new language. It is, according to the Gentleman in Act 4, Scene 5, 'unshaped' but moves those who hear it. She is no longer asking what she should think or say, as in Act 1, Scene 3. By Act 4, Scene 5 she can even demand that those around her, even the queen and king, actually listen to her: 'pray you mark'. Ophelia's tragedy is that she can only fully use her voice, when she is (in Claudius's words) 'Divided from herself and her fair judgement' *(Act 4, Scene 5)*.

Metaphor

Metaphors often link two things that are otherwise unrelated. For example, when Hamlet says that he will sit with Ophelia during the play scene in Act 3, Scene 2 because 'here's metal more attractive', he is comparing Ophelia with metal, in that she has magnetic power over him.

Shakespeare also uses metaphor to reveal more about characters. For example, when talking with Rosencrantz and Guildenstern in Act 3, Scene 2, Hamlet compares himself to a recorder, the musical instrument. He wants his one-time friends to understand why they should not try, and will not succeed, to find out what is really wrong with him. He complains that they see him simply as an instrument to 'play upon' and that they want to 'know my stops, you would pluck out the heart of my mystery, you would sound me from my lowest note to the top of my compass'. He goes on to say that, even though there is 'much music' in himself and the recorder, his so-called friends cannot 'make it speak'. Hamlet is using metaphor to show that he is not a mere thing, and that, similarly, he cannot be used.

There are many other examples of metaphors in the play.

Activity 9

Work out what is being compared in each of following metaphors from Hamlet's most famous 'To be or not to be' soliloquy, in Act 3, Scene 1.

a) take arms against a sea of troubles

b) The undiscover'd country

c) their currents turn awry.

Blank verse

Shakespeare uses **blank verse** in much of *Hamlet*. One of the many reasons that blank verse is so effective as a way of writing drama is because it mirrors the natural rhythms of English speech. In addition, although the **iambic beat** is its characteristic feature, there is plenty of room for variation. In fact, Shakespeare is particularly keen on breaking up the expected rhythm of blank verse and he uses this **metre** in a flexible way to make the lines sound more interesting, realistic and natural.

Here is an analysis of the metre of the beginning of Hamlet's most famous soliloquy (– shows an unstressed syllable, / a stressed syllable):

```
-  /  - /  - /  /   - -   /   -
```
To be, or not to be, that is the question:

```
/    - - /   - / - /   - / -
```
Whether 'tis nobler in the mind to suffer

```
-   /   -  / -  -  - /  -   /  -
```
The slings and arrows of outrageous fortune,

```
- -  /  /  - /  - /  - /   -
```
Or to take arms against a sea of troubles,

```
-   / -  / - /  -    - /  - /
```
And by opposing end them. To die – to sleep,

```
/ /   -  / - /  - /  -  /
```
No more; and by a sleep to say we end

```
-  /   -  -  -  /  -  / - -  /
```
The heart–ache and the thousand natural shocks

```
-   /  - /  - /  - /  - /  -
```
That flesh is heir to, 'tis a consummation

```
- /  - / - /    - / - /
```
Devoutly to be wish'd. To die, to sleep;

```
- /   -  /  - /     / /   - /
```
To sleep, perchance to dream – ay, there's the rub;

Shakespeare also uses metre to reveal character. In the previous quotation, there are five **weak (or 'feminine') endings** to lines. This could have the effect of showing Hamlet's uncertainty at this moment in the play. In addition, there are pauses, shown by punctuation in the soliloquy. This use of **caesura** is another way in which Shakespeare can indicate the movement of thought in Hamlet's mind.

Shakespeare also uses **rhyming couplets** occasionally, especially to close a scene, for example:

> **My words fly up, my thoughts remain below.**
> **Words without thoughts never to heaven go.**
> *(Claudius, Act 3, Scene 3)*

Activity 10

a) Identify all the moments in the opening lines of Hamlet's 'To be or not to be' soliloquy where Shakespeare changes the regular iambic stress pattern.

b) Then try to identify examples of the following different variations:

- **trochee**
- weak (or 'feminine') ending
- **spondee**.

Activity 11

Find other examples of Shakespeare ending a scene with a rhyming couplet. What is the dramatic effect in each case?

blank verse unrhymed verse; the five beats in each line are known as iambic pentameter

caesura a break or pause in a line of poetry

iambic beat rhythm in which the first syllable is unstressed and the second is stressed/emphasized, e.g. the word 'because' is always an iamb, with stress on the second syllable

metre the rhythm of a line of poetry

rhyming couplet a pair of lines in poetry that rhyme

spondee two stressed syllables together

trochee a strong syllable, followed by a weak one (reverse iamb)

weak (or 'feminine') ending a line of poetry with an extra, unstressed final syllable

Prose

At certain times in *Hamlet*, Shakespeare switches from blank verse to **prose**, sometimes within the same scene.

Characters who are, or who are pretending to be mad, usually use prose. (Shakespeare, however, also gives Ophelia rhyming songs in her madness and Hamlet offers occasional bursts of really bad poetry, usually when he is acting in a manic way.)

In contrast, however, some of the most serious and very calm lines spoken in *Hamlet* are in prose. The second example below is also written almost completely in **monosyllables**. Once again, Shakespeare shows us something about a character not only through *what* is said, but *how* they say it.

Key quotations

What piece of work is a man, how noble in reason, how infinite in faculties, in form and moving how express and admirable, in action how like an angel, in apprehension how like a god: the beauty of the world, the paragon of animals – and yet, to me, what is this quintessence of dust? *(Hamlet, Act 2, Scene 2)*

Not a whit. We defy augury. There is special providence in the fall of a sparrow. If it be now, 'tis not to come; if it be not to come, it will be now; if it be not now, yet it will come. The readiness is all. Since no man, of ought he leaves, knows aught, what is't to leave betimes? Let be. *(Hamlet, Act 5, Scene 2)*

Activity 12

a) Make a copy of the diagram on the next page. Add a note in each circle to say whether the lines are in **verse** or prose, then draw lines to link scenes with similar characteristics.

b) Write a paragraph summarizing your findings about the different occasions in which Shakespeare uses prose and why you think he does this.

---

monosyllable a word of one syllable

prose writing that is not poetry and usually written in ordinary language without obviously rhythmical structure

verse poetry

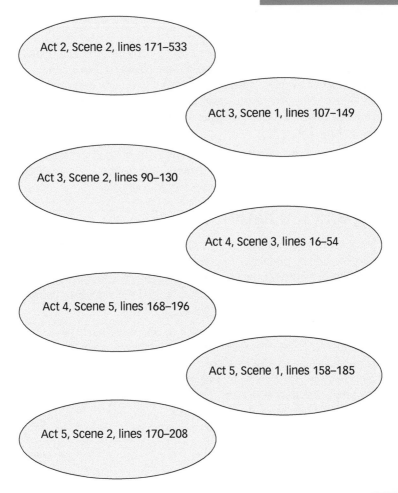

Act 2, Scene 2, lines 171–533

Act 3, Scene 1, lines 107–149

Act 3, Scene 2, lines 90–130

Act 4, Scene 3, lines 16–54

Act 4, Scene 5, lines 168–196

Act 5, Scene 1, lines 158–185

Act 5, Scene 2, lines 170–208

Writing about language

When examining Shakespeare's use of language, think about the dramatic context of the episode you are writing about so that you can work out the dramatic reason and the dramatic effect of the language he chooses.

It is important to show that you know, for example, that a particular scene is written in prose, or that a character uses a particular image repeatedly. However, you also need to analyse the reasons for the use of specific language and its effects in a critical way. Having identified a feature of Shakespeare's language, you might find it helpful to ask: So what? This forces you to explain the significance of the feature you have identified.

Themes

One of the reasons *Hamlet* has been performed for so many centuries (when many plays by Shakespeare's contemporaries, and even some plays by Shakespeare himself, have not) is that the play's themes are relevant to everyone and can be reinterpreted for each new generation. Death, love, revenge and family relationships are all timeless and universal topics, as relevant to a modern audience as they were in Shakespeare's own time.

But *Hamlet* does not just contain themes, it explores them, often in challenging and complex ways. Shakespeare uses his drama to make us think about mental illness, the supernatural, the divine and the nature of reality, for example.

Seeming and the nature of reality

Hamlet as a whole makes us question what is real and what is not. Some of the questions are answered by the play. For example, at first it seems that Claudius is a capable, confident leader who only wants the best for his 'son' Hamlet, as he calls him in Act 1, Scene 2. The play reveals that in reality he is a 'smiling damned villain', as Hamlet calls Claudius in Act 1, Scene 5.

But other questions, about reality and what seems to be, remain much harder to answer. Is the Ghost real? Is Hamlet really mad? Did Hamlet really love Ophelia? Shakespeare represents the Danish royal court as a place where no one is quite what they seem, a place where characters say one thing, while secretly thinking another. One of the major themes of *Hamlet* is, therefore, seeming (appearing to be real or genuine, but not necessarily being so).

Hamlet himself is preoccupied with this idea.

> **Key quotation**
>
> I know not 'seems'.
> 'Tis not alone my inky cloak, good mother [...]
> Together with all forms, moods, shapes of grief,
> That can denote me truly. These indeed seem,
> For they are actions that a man might play;
> But I have that within which passes show,
> These but the trappings and the suits of woe.
> (Hamlet, Act 1, Scene 2)

He insists that outward behaviour or dress only takes one so far in understanding a human being. These things can only show a certain amount of what truly lies inside a person. He finds it painful that there is so much within him that he cannot show. As he says later, when challenging Rosencrantz and Guildenstern, who are trying to 'play upon' him as if he were a musical instrument, he has much 'music' in him, but he will not give up what is within him easily *(Act 3, Scene 2)*.

When Hamlet says he 'knows not "seems"' in Act 1, Scene 2, he sets himself apart from everyone else in two ways. First of all, he is saying that there is so much going on inside him that it is impossible for his behaviour to 'denote' him truly. But he is also comparing himself (a man of true feeling) with an actor, who simply puts on the 'trappings and suits of woe' (the external signs), an early indication of another important theme in the play – acting.

Activity 1

Annotate a copy of Act 2, Scene 2, from the beginning of the scene up to the queen's line 'Ay, Amen', to show not what the character is actually saying but the **subtext** that they might really be *thinking*.

subtext the implicit or underlying meaning

Theatre and acting

Acting is significant to *Hamlet* both in terms of people being false (Claudius acts a part throughout the play) but also in the sense of theatre. The Players have an important part to play and drama is one of Hamlet's passions. When the Players arrive, he welcomes them as old friends. Hamlet decides, having become upset about an actor's performance of grief, to use theatre to test the truth of what the Ghost says.

There is, of course, an irony at work here. The Ghost might be an illusion (a piece of theatre) created by the Devil in order to 'abuse' Hamlet, as he himself fears in Act 2, Scene 2, but Hamlet intends to use theatre to find out if the Ghost is an illusion.

Hamlet himself also becomes an actor, putting on what he tells Horatio is a fake madness. One of most interesting questions raised by the play is whether that role takes him over.

Activity 2

Which of the following characters put on an act at some point during the play? When and why do they do so? To what extent do your findings suggest the importance of acting as a theme in *Hamlet*?

- Hamlet
- Claudius
- Ophelia
- Gertrude
- Rosencrantz
- Horatio

The play-within-a-play

At the centre of Shakespeare's play is the formal performance of a play, complete with onstage audience. 'The Mousetrap' creates certain effects, besides proving Claudius's guilt:

- The audience sees the players performing long speeches in an unnatural way. This makes the main action of *Hamlet* seem more real and naturalistic.

- The use of the play-within-a-play structure allows Shakespeare to explore further the theme of seeming. For example, Hamlet is disturbed that the actor can cry real tears and move his audience. In contrast, Hamlet is not only unable to express his own feelings, but he cannot communicate those feelings to others.

- The audience is made to think about acting and all the other characters who put on an act.

In 'The Mousetrap', we, the audience, see a play performed within a play. Specifically, we watch Hamlet watching Claudius watching the play, which prompts us to think about what happens when we watch a play.

In *Hamlet*, Shakespeare makes the audience think about the idea of acting and 'playing', and what happens when we watch a play.

Activity 3

Imagine that you are each of the following characters. Write a couple of lines as each character, about your response to 'The Mousetrap' before, during and after its performance, using language from the text.

a) Claudius

d) Gertrude

b) Hamlet

e) Polonius

c) Ophelia

f) Horatio

Tips for assessment

You will be displaying a high level of critical response to the play if you explore *Hamlet* as metatheatre, a term that refers to self-reflexive plays, or – theatre about theatre. Metatheatre reminds audiences that a play is, in fact, a play and the playwright therefore draws attention to theatre as a fiction and challenges dramatic realism.

The play-within-a-play in *Hamlet* is an obvious example of metatheatre but, on a deeper level, the play's preoccupation with playing, stages, acting and fictions makes the audience see life itself as essentially theatrical. As one of Shakespeare's other melancholic characters, Jacques in *As You Like It*, says: 'All the world's a stage, and all the men and women merely players'.

Fathers

Claudius says, 'think of us / As of a father' to Hamlet in Act 1, Scene 2. It seems unlikely Hamlet will do that given his **pun** on 'son' and 'sun': 'too much in the sun'. One reason is that Hamlet, as we soon find out, is disgusted with his mother for marrying Claudius so quickly. Another reason for Hamlet's hostility towards Claudius is that the prince hero-worships his real father.

> **pun** a play on words

Hamlet and Old Hamlet

The critic Laurie Maguire argues that Hamlet's view of his father is a sign that he is trapped in the early stages of grief, which involves idealization of the dead person. What Maguire calls the 'extreme bifurcation' (the division of something into two parts) between Old Hamlet and Claudius actually 'flies in the face of the evidence, for the Ghost refers to his sins and imperfections and, if we except his regicide, Claudius can, in production, seem every inch the statesman'.

Hamlet sees himself as very different from his father, but in one way they are very similar. When the Ghost speaks to Hamlet in Act 1, Scene 5, he becomes very focused on the sexual activities of his 'seeming-virtuous queen' and forgets, for a while at least, to tell Hamlet what Claudius has actually done. Similarly, Hamlet will get distracted from his grief for his father by his disgust at his mother's sexual activities, which dominates his opening soliloquy in Act 1, Scene 2, even before he has heard the Ghost speak.

Activity 4

Imagine you are casting the role of Old Hamlet. You need to create a character profile for potential actors. List four or five points that need to go into the profile, highlighting which have been taken from Hamlet's descriptions of his father.

Polonius as a father

Polonius is the other significant father in *Hamlet*. It is hard to decide whether he is a good father. On the one hand, he gives Laertes some good if lengthy advice in Act 1, Scene 3, including one of the most famous lines from the play: 'to thine own self be true'. He is also protective towards Ophelia, concerned that Hamlet is motivated only by lust ('blood'), and he tells her, 'Do not believe his vows' (*Act 1, Scene 3*).

Both Laertes and Ophelia are, it seems, completely obedient to their father, although Ophelia has to stay in Elsinore, while Laertes can escape to France. Polonius sends a spy to Paris to find out if Laertes has been drinking, fencing, swearing, quarrelling or womanizing. He even says that Reynaldo, the spy, should spread rumours that Laertes is doing all these things, in order to find out the truth. Polonius then makes Ophelia lie for him and spies on her when she talks with Hamlet.

Activity 5

Explain to what extent you think Polonius is a good father, using evidence from the text to support your opinion.

Patriarchy and the divine right of kings

Fathers were important in Shakespeare's time because of widely held beliefs about **patriarchy**. (For more on men's power, see page 28).

When King James came to the throne in 1603, he presented himself as a father to his people. He had the Bible to back him up. As one theorist of the time wrote, not only Adam but all following leaders of mankind 'had by right of fatherhood, royal authority over their children'. Indeed, the fifth of the Ten Commandments in the Bible, 'Honour thy father…', demanded respect for those in authority generally, from the father up to the king. The superior, all-powerful and, crucially, God-given position of the father/king was, therefore, absolutely accepted. Obedience was the only possible response, even if the father/king behaved badly.

The political application of these ideas is known as the divine right of kings. This belief that kings and queens have a God-given right to rule was upheld by the Church and rebellion against the monarch was therefore regarded as a sin.

These ideas make it is easier to understand why Ophelia obeys her father Polonius. In addition, one of the many reasons Hamlet has such a problem with revenge is that it would mean killing his king. If Claudius's killing of Old Hamlet has the 'primal eldest curse' upon it (as Claudius admits in his soliloquy in Act 3, Scene 3), then killing one's king on the word of a Ghost who might or might not be the devil is almost as bad.

> **patriarchy** a way of organizing life (political, religious, social or personal) so that men have power, including over women, justified in Shakespeare's time by the Bible

Death

The theme of death is explored by Shakespeare in many different ways, in addition to being the play's basic plot driver.

Hamlet thinks long and hard about what happens when we die. The Ghost's very existence forces even more questions about the matter. Over the course of the play we see one character contemplate suicide. Another (perhaps) commits suicide: **'Her death was doubtful'**, we are told of Ophelia in Act 5, Scene 1. We also hear that twenty thousand men **'Go to their graves like beds'** in Act 4, Scene 4. Shakespeare contrasts the mass deaths of war with the individual deaths in Elsinore. We see a random killing and hear of pre-meditated killings.

As you saw when considering the graveyard scene from different perspectives (look back at pages 36 and 56), Shakespeare uses comedy to reflect on the biblical lines, 'dust thou art, and unto dust shalt thou return'. Gertrude makes a similar reference to dust in the court scene at the start of the play, when she suggests that Hamlet's mourning for his father is too extreme:

> **Key quotation**
>
> Do not for ever with thy vailed lids
> Seek for thy noble father in the dust.
> Thou know'st 'tis common: all that lives must die,
> Passing through nature to eternity.
> *(Gertrude, Act 1, Scene 2)*

The imagery of death runs through the play, culminating in Fortinbras's personification of a hungry death preparing to feast on the bodies covering the stage:

> **Key quotation**
>
>   O proud Death,
> What feast is toward in thine eternal cell,
> That thou so many princes at a shot
> So bloodily hast struck?
> *(Fortinbras, Act 5, Scene 2)*

Shakespeare explores many aspects of death, including how grief works. Even before Hamlet is told that his father has returned as a ghost, he is utterly preoccupied with him: **'My father – methinks I see my father'**, he tells Horatio in Act 1, Scene 2, before reassuring his friend that he sees his father in his **'mind's eye'**. Shakespeare also draws attention to the ways in which people honour and remember the dead – or, indeed, dishonour and fail to remember them.

After Hamlet leaves Elsinore, he encounters death in three different forms:

- Fortinbras's army
- the gravediggers and Yorick's skull
- Ophelia's burial.

Perhaps the play records Hamlet's journey to understanding, or at least accepting, the inevitability of death.

David Tennant's Hamlet contemplates death in the Royal Shakespeare Company production at The Courtyard Theatre, London, 2008

Activity 6

Copy and complete the following table to suggest what Hamlet learns from his various encounters with death after he leaves Elsinore.

Incident	Quotation	What Hamlet learns about death
Fortinbras's army		
Yorick's skull		
Ophelia's burial		

Revenge

In terms of genre and plot, *Hamlet* is a revenge tragedy (see page 34), but Shakespeare also makes the audience think about the theme of revenge and consider questions about who has the right to take vengeance.

Even before Hamlet hears the Ghost's story, he is concerned that something terrible has happened: he suspects **'foul play'** as early as Act 1, Scene 2. At this stage, Hamlet believes that hidden crimes will be revealed: **'Foul deeds will rise, / Though all the earth o'erwhelm them, to men's eyes.'** This is very similar to the popular saying, 'murder will out', but it raises another question: If foul deeds will eventually be revealed, is this through divine intervention? If so, should humans wait for that divine intervention, rather than take vengeance into their own hands? Once again, Shakespeare seems to pose as many questions as he answers.

The deaths at the end of the play can be seen as a form of justice to restore order. Laertes is killed by the poison he intended for Hamlet. Claudius dies by the rapier and by poison, leading Laertes to comment **'He is justly serv'd'** *(Act 5, Scene 2)*.

However, what justice is there in the queen's death from the poison intended for Hamlet? Or in Hamlet's own death? These questions are hard to answer, especially as Shakespeare does not provide the audience with any ready-made answers.

Madness

We may use different words to describe mental illness today, but it is clear that 'madness' is one of the most important themes in Hamlet.

In Act 1, Scene 4 Horatio fears that the Ghost will 'draw' Hamlet 'into madness' and 'deprive' him of the 'sovereignty of reason'. This is something that does actually happen to Ophelia as she is 'Divided from herself and her fair judgement' in Act 4, Scene 5.

For Claudius, as for Shakespeare's contemporaries, it was reason, rationality and judgement that separated humans from beasts, and men had more reason, rationality and judgement than women.

> **Key quotations**
>
> Madness in great ones must not unwatch'd go.
> (Claudius, Act 3, Scene 1)
>
> I like him not, nor stands it safe with us
> To let his madness range.
> (Claudius, Act 3, Scene 3)
>
> Divided from herself and her fair judgement,
> Without the which we are pictures, or mere beasts;
> (Claudius, Act 4, Scene 5)

Shakespeare returns to this idea at the very end of the play. In the last scene, Hamlet gives a long speech about his 'madness' just before his fencing match with Laertes, arguing that he can separate himself from his own madness.

> **Key quotation**
>
> What I have done
> That might your nature, honour, and exception
> Roughly awake, I here proclaim was madness.
> Was't Hamlet wrong'd Laertes? Never Hamlet.
> If Hamlet from himself be ta'en away,
> And when he's not himself does wrong Laertes,
> Then Hamlet does it not, Hamlet denies it.
> Who does it then? His madness. If't be so,
> Hamlet is of the faction that is wrong'd;
> His madness is poor Hamlet's enemy.
> (Hamlet, Act 5, Scene 2)

Madness is also important to the play because, paradoxically, truth can emerge through it. Madness can hit on things that reason and sanity miss, as Polonius comments on Hamlet's words in Act 2, Scene 2: **'Though this be madness, yet there is method in 't.'** (However, there may be method in Hamlet's madness because he may be playing a part in order to pursue his revenge; in Act 3, Scene 1, Guildenstern accuses him of a **'crafty madness'**.) The idea of truth emerging from madness reappears in the representation of Ophelia.

> **Key quotation**
>
> she may strew
> **Dangerous conjectures in ill-breeding minds**
> *(Horatio, Act 4, Scene 5)*

What is certain is that whether the madness in Hamlet or Ophelia is real or not, it is seen as dangerous, both socially and politically. Madness is represented as a lack of order in the mind, and that disorder suggests political disorder, feared by the monarchy in Shakespeare's time and by the characters in Hamlet (see the quotation from King James on page 87).

Activity 7

Imagine Hamlet is on trial for killing Polonius and he is delivering his speech about madness from Act 5, Scene 2 in a court of law. In trying to prove him guilty, what questions might the prosecutor ask Hamlet about the claims he makes in this speech? How would Hamlet justify what he says? Write an imagined dialogue between the two.

Women's frailties

The way women are presented in *Hamlet* presents significant challenges for modern audiences. It could be argued that Gertrude and Ophelia are merely passive victims caught in the cross-fire of the revenge plot controlled by the male characters. Although female characters are allowed to respond, report and occasionally plead, Shakespeare rarely shows them thinking or rationally discussing and interpreting situations.

Alice Patten's Ophelia is subjected to Ed Stoppard's Hamlet's abuse in this 2005 English Touring Company production

Instead they are told what to think, what to do and – most importantly – what they are. For example, in Act 1, Scene 3, Laertes tells Ophelia starkly that she is a fool to believe Hamlet loves her and to **'Think it no more.'** In the same scene, Polonius tells her that she has been behaving like a **'green girl'** and a **'baby'** in accepting Hamlet's offer of love and that she must remember she is his daughter and behave according to his command, not her own judgement or feelings. Later, in Act 3, Scene 1, Hamlet continues in the same vein, telling Ophelia that **'wise men know well enough what monsters you [women] make of them'**, whilst accusing her of being little more than a prostitute.

It is not surprising that interpretations of the play have traditionally been strongly influenced by Hamlet's view of his mother. Indeed, he is one of Gertrude's harshest critics. Even when, in Act 1, Scene 5, the Ghost has expressly told Hamlet to **'Leave her to heaven'**, he still insults his mother (**'O most pernicious woman!'**) before he curses Claudius, the **'damned villain'**. Hamlet is obsessed with Gertrude's sexual activity and, in the closet scene, he tells her how disgusted he is by her sexual desires. He is also extremely critical of her lack of judgement and that she cannot seem to see a difference between Claudius and Old Hamlet. He says that she is motivated by lust and he cannot believe that she could let this blind her. His tirade is only interrupted by the reappearance of the Ghost, who is also sure that women are weak: **'Conceit in weakest bodies strongest works'** *(Act 3, Scene 4)*. Hamlet may be calmer after the Ghost's intervention, but he still tells his mother what to do: she must not let **'the bloat king tempt'** her into bed again *(Act 3, Scene 4)*.

There may be only two female characters in *Hamlet*, but there is a lot of talk about women in general. From Hamlet's comment in his first soliloquy in Act 1, Scene 2 (**'Frailty, thy name is woman'**) to the moment when he turns Ophelia's comment on the short prologue to 'The Mousetrap' into a judgement on the brevity of **'woman's love'** *(Act 3, Scene 2)*, there are many occasions when a female character or the nature of women in general is apparently defined by one of the male characters.

Overall, Hamlet talks much more about his mother (and about women) than Gertrude talks about herself. Shakespeare does not give Gertrude her own soliloquy, so the audience is even more swayed by Hamlet's powerful language.

Activity 8

'*Hamlet* as a whole shows that Hamlet's claim, **'Frailty, thy name is woman'**, is true.' Write a paragraph or two arguing for or against this view.

Tips for assessment

If you are asked to write about women in *Hamlet*, you can give more depth to your essay by discussing how ideas about women in general (as well as the individual female characters) are presented in the play.

Masculinity and heroism

Hamlet is the hero of a revenge tragedy, or tragedy of blood. The avenger in a conventional revenge tragedy is the sort of man who will 'sweep to my revenge' *(Act 1, Scene 5)* and 'drink hot blood', to quote Hamlet at the end of Act 3, Scene 2. However, when we first meet Hamlet, all he wants to do is go back to university. He is very much an intellectual and he seems to be suffering from depression, or what Shakespeare called melancholy. The only violence he considers is against himself, and he rejects even that as being against God's will. He is absolutely not the man of action that an audience watching a revenge tragedy might have been expecting. Hamlet knows this. In his first soliloquy, he says, 'My father's brother – but no more like my father / Than I to Hercules' *(Act 1, Scene 2)*. At this stage in the play, he is not too concerned about his complete lack of traditional heroic qualities. Then again, he has not yet seen the Ghost or been told to become a revenger.

Activity 9

Who was Hercules? Carry out some research about him. Write a list of ways in which Hamlet is *not* like him.

As the play progresses, Hamlet becomes more and more troubled by what he perceives as his own cowardice and weakness. He sees these as evidence of his own dangerous femininity. Perhaps the seed of doubt was sown by Claudius accusing him of 'unmanly' grief in the opening court scene. What is certain is that when Hamlet's self-hatred is expressed, he uses **gendered language**.

Activity 10

a) Using a good dictionary, investigate the slang meanings of the words 'whore', 'drab' and 'scullion', which Hamlet uses about himself in his soliloquy at the end of Act 2, Scene 2. Suggest some modern equivalents for each of them.

b) What does the use of these words tell you about Hamlet?

Shakespeare brings together the themes of women and masculinity at the end of the play. First Laertes, then Hamlet, refer to 'woman' when talking about an emotion they are experiencing.

> **gendered language** language that identifies something as either masculine or feminine

Activity 11

Examine the following two quotations.

- **When these are gone, / The woman will be out.** (*Laertes, Act 4, Scene 7*)
- **It is but foolery, but it is such a kind of gaingiving as would perhaps trouble a woman.** (*Hamlet, Act 5, Scene 2*)

What do they tell you about each man's beliefs about women?

Politics

The Fortinbras subplot is the most obvious political (or military) element in *Hamlet*, but politics is extremely relevant to the tragedy in Elsinore. You can find out more about the way in which some productions have made *Hamlet* into a political play in the chapter on Performance (see page 84).

Prince Hamlet and Danish politics

However much Hamlet wants to forget that he is a prince (and return to his studies in Wittenberg), the play does not let *us* forget it.

Laertes provides an early insight into the ways in which Hamlet is trapped by his royal birth, telling Ophelia in Act 1, Scene 3 that although it is possible that Hamlet loves her now, in reality 'his will is not his own'. Princes cannot choose their brides. Laertes explains that Hamlet's choice is 'circumscrib'd / Unto the voice and yielding of that body / Whereof he is the head'.

Laertes's words are a reminder of the particular political system operating in Shakespeare's Denmark. It is an *elected* monarchy, a system in which the king is elected, in contrast to hereditary monarchy. Shakespeare may have presented Denmark as an elected monarchy because, if the country had mirrored the English hereditary system, Hamlet would have inherited the throne automatically on the death of his father and Claudius would have been a usurper, with no entitlement to it. Hamlet would have been completely justified in removing Claudius to become the rightful king himself. However, with the elected system, Claudius seems to have cheated Hamlet of his chance to be elected as king by moving so quickly; Hamlet complains to Horatio that Claudius has 'Popp'd in between th'election and my hopes' (*Act 5, Scene 2*).

Activity 12

In Act 1, Scene 3, Shakespeare includes a reference to 'the main voice of Denmark', showing the importance of the people's support (voice) in politics and maintaining power. Read through Scenes 5 and 7 in Act 4 in which the people (described as the 'general gender', *Act 4, Scene 7*, or 'Danes') are mentioned. What do you learn about the Danish people from these scenes?

A political tragedy?

The play's title in Shakespeare's time was 'The Tragical History of Hamlet, Prince of Denmark'. This reminds us that it is the tragedy of a country as much as of an individual. In 1595, Sir Philip Sidney, (1554–1586), an English writer and soldier, wrote in general terms about tragedy as a literary genre:

> the high and excellent Tragedy, that opens the greatest wounds, and shows forth the ulcers that are covered with tissue; that makes kings fear to be tyrants [cruel and unjust rulers], and tyrants manifest [reveal] their tyrannical humours; that, with stirring the affects [responses] of admiration and commiseration [pity], teaches the uncertainty of this world, and upon how weak foundations gilden [golden] roofs are built
>
> (Sir Philip Sidney, 'The Defence of Poesy')

Does this theory apply to *Hamlet*? Sidney argues that tragedy opens up 'the greatest wounds' and uncovers the 'ulcers' beneath the surface of society. *Hamlet* certainly reveals something very **'rotten in the state of Denmark'** (as the guard Marcellus expresses it in Act 1, Scene 4) and the play is full of images of illness and disease. Whether watching the play would make a real tyrant question or stop his tyranny, in Shakespeare's or our own time, is a debatable question.

Activity 13

Which parts of the quotation from Sir Philip Sidney refer to the following ideas about tragedy?

a) Tragedy can work to expose hidden evil in political life.

b) Kings will think twice about acting tyrannically because audiences will see what happens to evil leaders.

c) Tragedy will show audiences that even the most powerful people can fall because that is the nature of the world.

The personal and the political

At the start of the play, Hamlet thinks he can leave Elsinore and find his own way through the mire of corruption at the Danish court by holding his tongue even if his heart is breaking, keeping **'that within which passeth show'** *(Act 1, Scene 2)*. He rejects the political world of Denmark.

However, a vital turning point in the political drama comes when Ophelia is being laid to rest in Act 5, Scene 1. Hamlet surprises everyone by bursting onto the scene, when Claudius believes he is either still on his way to England or already dead. Suddenly, it seems as if Hamlet is laying claim to the throne of Denmark when he says **'This is I, / Hamlet the Dane'** because 'the Dane' would usually be understood to mean king of Denmark (Act 5, Scene 1). It is possible to argue that by the end of the play Hamlet embraces his public identity and his public duty, both as a son and as a prince.

The final scene, strewn with dead bodies, including Hamlet played by Kenneth Branagh, in the Royal Shakespeare Company production at the Barbican Theatre, London, 1992

The lack of soliloquies from Hamlet in the later parts of the play underlines this transition. His final speeches, in Act 5, Scene 2, are dominated by a sense of audience and of being unable to speak truly for himself: **'tell my story [...] the rest is silence'**. The one thing he is able to do is to give his **'dying voice'** to support Fortinbras, a public and political act.

Quickly and efficiently, Horatio asks for **'these bodies / High on a stage be placed to the view'**. He is going to control how the world sees the tragedy. He is relieved that Fortinbras is going to take political control, because he fears more trouble, if **'men's minds are wild'**.

Shakespeare ends the play with Fortinbras providing a public, military, heroic vision of Hamlet's life and death. There is a painful irony in the way that the external displays of mourning, which Hamlet rejected as inadequate in his very first scene (the **'customary suits of solemn black'**) because they could not **'denote him truly'** *(Act 1, Scene 2)*, dominate the end of the play.

Writing about themes

Once you have identified which theme you are being asked to write about, you will need to demonstrate *how* the theme is presented. Always bear in mind that the theme is being explored dramatically and try to relate your discussion of it to the play as a whole. You should demonstrate:

- how the theme is presented in the beginning, middle and end of the play (and/or in performance)
- why the theme is important to the play as a whole.

Since its first performance, probably in 1601, each generation has created its own interpretation of *Hamlet*, and the play is now a global phenomenon, transplanted to cultures and languages far removed from its birthplace in the Globe Theatre in London, over four hundred years ago.

Hamlet in Shakespeare's time: the Globe Theatre

In Shakespeare's time, people from all parts of society went to the theatre. The general public would pay a penny to stand close to the stage and interact with the actors. Richer people would pay to sit in the galleries, bringing cushions to make the wooden seats more comfortable. The theatre had no roof and plays were performed in daylight. The stage was covered in straw and measured approximately 13 metres wide by 8 metres from front to back.

Shakespeare's actors had to compete against the noise of the crowd, who shouted, hurled fruit and sometimes attempted to join in with the performance on the stage.

The wall across the back of the stage had a door at each end for entrances and exits, and a central opening that was normally concealed by hangings. Above the stage there was a trapdoor and a windlass, which lowered performers onto the stage. In the centre of the stage was a trapdoor into which characters could descend or be lowered or from which they could emerge.

The modern Globe Theatre, in London, opened in 1997 as a replica of the original Elizabethan theatre

It seems that there was usually a creative working relationship between the playwright and performers. Indeed, Shakespeare was both a playwright and an actor. There are very few stage directions in the published versions of his plays. Most of the stage directions you have in your modern copy were added by editors.

Playwrights created their characters with certain actors in mind. For example, Richard Burbage worked in the same company as Shakespeare for many years and the playwright created many parts, including in *Richard III* (an early play) and *Hamlet*, for the actor.

Activity 1

a) Make a list of differences between theatre in Shakespeare's time and theatre now.

b) Think of some ways in which a performance of *Hamlet* would be different now to how it would have been when Shakespeare was writing. For example, in Shakespeare's time, the Ghost would probably have appeared from the trapdoor beneath the stage. Today, in a modern theatre, there are many other ways in which to stage the Ghost's scenes.

Hamlet in the 18th and 19th centuries

In the century after Shakespeare's death, the Fortinbras plot was cut out completely. This indicates that the personal tragedy of Hamlet, rather than the political, national issues in the play, interested audiences most. The most famous actor of the 18th century, David Garrick, performed Hamlet as an extremely emotional but always good man. Throughout, Garrick's Hamlet was motivated by his love for his father, even sobbing in his grief.

By the late 19th century, the most famous Hamlet was the actor Henry Irving. In contrast to Garrick, Irving played up the character's volatility. His was a changeable, unpredictable Hamlet and, most importantly, it was hard to tell if Irving's Hamlet was truly mad or only pretending to be so.

Activity 2

David Garrick chose to cut the Fortinbras scenes, the scene in which Hamlet sends Rosencrantz and Guildenstern to their deaths, and Hamlet's soliloquy when he decides not to kill Claudius. Write a paragraph identifying what aspects you think Garrick did *not* want in the play and in the character of Hamlet.

Hamlet in the 20ᵗʰ and 21ˢᵗ centuries

Freudian *Hamlet*

In 1937, another great actor, Laurence Olivier, took the psychological interpretation of the play even further. His performance was strongly influenced by the work of the psychoanalyst, Sigmund Freud (see page 93). Applied to Shakespeare's *Hamlet*, Freud's theory of the Oedipus complex provides an underlying, but unacknowledged, reason for Hamlet's delay. In this interpretation the prince cannot bring himself to kill Claudius because his uncle has actually fulfilled what Hamlet subconsciously desires, which is sex with his mother.

The most obvious result of this interpretation in performance is to make the relationship between *Hamlet* and Gertrude more significant, and highly sexualized. For years after Olivier, many productions of *Hamlet* were influenced by Freudian interpretation. In 2015, for example, David Tennant's Hamlet confronted Gertrude by standing astride her on her bed.

Political *Hamlet*

Another important tradition of *Hamlet* performance in the 20ᵗʰ century focused on the political elements in the play, taking attention away from individual, family and sexual matters.

The playwright Bertolt Brecht, writing in the 1930s, insisted that we should see the play historically, rather than psychologically. Brecht saw Hamlet caught between two worlds and two eras. He thought it significant that Hamlet is a student at Wittenberg, which was a Protestant university. His studies would have taught him to value reason and conscience, but in Elsinore these things are worthless, because it is a world that operates by feudal values and violence. For Brecht, Hamlet's tragedy does not lie within him, but around him. He is a new kind of man, stranded in a medieval society.

Another famous example of a political interpretation of *Hamlet* is the 1964 black and white Soviet Russian film version directed by Grigori Kozintsev.

Kozintsev's *Hamlet*, in Russian, is as much about political and public turmoil as it is about personal turmoil

A stage production in 1988, starring Kenneth Branagh, made Fortinbras's arrival at the end of the play a crucial part of the tragedy. Fortinbras's command in the play's last line to 'Go, bid the soldiers shoot' prompted his armed guard to immediately kill Horatio and any Danish lord left standing.

A political reading of *Hamlet* is, in some ways, as appropriate to Shakespeare's time as our own. King James I, who came to the throne in 1603, wrote that a king was like 'one set on a stage, whose smallest actions and gestures, all the people gazingly do behold'. The king is therefore seen as an actor on a stage, watched carefully by his people who see when the king makes an error. Any glimpse of a slip by a king on the political stage can be the 'mother of rebellion and disorder'.

Modernizing *Hamlet*

In 1925, *Hamlet* was performed in what was then modern dress at the Birmingham Repertory Theatre. Although the production seemed shockingly contemporary to the audience then, the idea behind the production was actually to try to be more loyal to the way in which *Hamlet* would have been performed in Shakespeare's time, since the actors in the 1600s would have been wearing the fashions of the time (for example, Ophelia mentions Hamlet's doublet and stockings in Act 2, Scene 1). In addition, in 1925, as in 1601, there were no breaks between the scenes, which was very different to 19th-century productions when there might be long pauses to change the scenery. The whole play was therefore considerably speeded up.

In a famous performance by the Royal Shakespeare Company in 1965, David Warner portrayed Hamlet as a restless, angry student, capturing the atmosphere of the sixties. This Hamlet appealed to young audiences, which cheered him on. Warner's Hamlet was not a withdrawn, moody intellectual but someone engaged in rebellion against the corrupt world of the older generation represented by Claudius and Polonius.

More recently, Michael Almereyda's film version of *Hamlet* in 2000 has Ethan Hawke playing the prince as an upper-middle-class dropout and amateur filmmaker. In this version, 'The Mousetrap' becomes a film by Hamlet. It is a home movie, obviously put together by Hamlet, with clips from old films and TV shows, and is screened in Claudius's home cinema. Almereyda therefore updates the idea of a play-within-a-play into a film-within-a-film.

Activity 3

a) Suggest a modern setting for *Hamlet*. You can choose anywhere you think will work, so long as it is set in today's world.

b) Write a paragraph to explain your ideas.

c) Find evidence from the text to support your ideas.

Ophelia in performance

Through much of the 19th century, Ophelia was played as a sweet, innocent young girl. Her death was a favourite topic for artists of the period and is portrayed as peaceful and beautiful.

Gradually, however, a more disturbing portrayal of Ophelia emerged. The celebrated Victorian actress Ellen Terry made Ophelia's mad scenes upsetting for the audience. The 1925 Birmingham Repertory Theatre production, mentioned on page 87, went further. It made Ophelia's mad scenes more sexually charged and made the obscene references in her songs explicit to the audience. By the 1970s, Ophelia had become a graphic 'dramatic study of mental pathology, even schizophrenia, sucking her thumb, headbanging, even drooling', according to the critic, Elaine Showalter.

Underlying this interpretation was a new concern with psychology and, in particular, the new idea of suppression. Ophelia, in madness, could express all the emotions and desires that she had been forced to suppress by the men in her life. (The idea of suppression is also important to Freudian interpretations of Hamlet's behaviour, as discussed on page 93.)

Ophelia, painted in 1852 by John Everett Millais

The performance of Ophelia's two scenes with Hamlet, in which he abuses and humiliates her, have also changed over time. The director has to decide how aggressive to make these scenes. Some will make Hamlet's abuse of Ophelia merely verbal. Others will make it physical. It is rare for a production to show Ophelia fighting back in any way, verbally or physically, because there are no clues in the text to suggest that she does.

Activity 4

Look carefully at the two images of Ophelia (the painting by Millais and the photo of Helena Bonham Carter).

a) Identify quotations from the play which illustrate these images of the life and death of Ophelia.

b) Is this easier for one of the images than the other? Why do you think that is?

From text to performance

Shakespeare was writing at a time when stage directions, if they were provided at all, were very basic. However, he does give clues to actors on how to perform their parts through the speeches and responses of others. For example, in Act 4, Scene 5, he makes sure that the actor playing Ophelia knows what to do because the Gentleman describes her behaviour: she should be 'distract', speak 'things in doubt / That carry but half sense' and use 'winks and nods and gestures'.

Helena Bonham Carter in the 1990 film *Hamlet*

Sometimes, focusing on the way in which a small detail could or should be performed can provide a key to the whole play. Take, for example, Hamlet's first lines in Act 1, Scene 2 'A little more than kin, and less than kind' and 'Not so, my lord, I am too much in the sun', both witty puns. Different productions perform these lines in different ways, while some productions cut them entirely. Consider these interpretations:

- If Hamlet stands apart from the rest of the characters, it shows that he is isolated, whether by choice or necessity. Does Claudius even hear Hamlet's words?
- The actor could speak the lines as asides to the audience. This establishes a close relationship between hero and audience, cutting across and undermining the stage authority of Claudius.
- The lines can be spoken directly, and rudely, to Claudius. This makes Hamlet less of an outsider, but also more makes him more of a problem for the king.
- The actor needs to decide whether to show anger, wit, desperation, grief or cynicism – or all of these reactions.
- The lines can be cut entirely, in which case Hamlet's first lines will probably be 'Ay, madam, it is common', addressed to his mother. This not only focuses attention on the mother/son relationship, but also cuts Claudius out of the conversation even more effectively.

Activity 5

Watch three film versions of the moment in Act 1, Scene 2 when Hamlet speaks his first words. Make sure you know exactly what the director has cut or changed.

a) Explain how each version establishes Hamlet's character through these opening shots and words.

b) Which version do you think is most consistent with the original text and which is most powerful as drama?

To be or not to be

Hamlet's famous 'To be, or not to be' speech in Act 3, Scene 1 is usually performed as a traditional soliloquy (see page 58). However, a careful analysis of the text suggests that Hamlet might know that he is being watched. In a production, the actor may notice Polonius and Claudius hiding, without them knowing he has seen them.

If this idea is followed through, then Hamlet is performing the speech mainly for the benefit of Claudius and Polonius. Suddenly, Hamlet's expressed desire to kill himself seems less genuine. Perhaps he is making sure that the king is convinced that he is indeed mad and therefore no threat to him. It's also possible that, knowing that Claudius can hear every word, Hamlet's question as to why anyone puts up with 'Th' oppressor's wrong' when it's possible to solve all one's problems with a 'bare bodkin' could be interpreted as a veiled threat to Claudius (*Act 3, Scene 1*).

Similarly, Hamlet's lines soon after, when he is talking with Ophelia in Act 3, Scene 1 ('I say we will have no more marriage. Those that are married already – all but one – shall live; the rest shall keep as they are') can also be understood as a threat to the king.

Finally, when Hamlet asks Ophelia, 'Where's your father?', she lies to him, saying 'At home, my lord' (*Act 3, Scene 1*). If the scene is played with Hamlet knowing exactly where Polonius and the king are, then he knows that she is lying, yet another psychological blow to the suffering prince.

The length of the play

Hamlet is Shakespeare's longest play, with over 4,000 lines and a running time of up to four hours. It is therefore unsurprising that stage or film directors decide to make cuts, although no cuts were made in Kenneth Branagh's 1996 film and the running time was 242 minutes!

Activity 6

Imagine you are a theatre director and need to cut down the running time of *Hamlet* for performance. You decide that much of the scene introducing the Players can go. But how much of Act 2, Scene 2 (from line 210 to 531) could you remove, without losing something that is crucial to plot or character?

a) On a copy of the scene, mark up what needs to stay.

b) Then compare your choices with a partner, justifying each decision.

Writing about performance

It can be tempting to write about Hamlet as if it is a novel. However, exploring the play in performance is vital if you are to keep focused on it as tragic drama. Make sure you:

* See as many productions of the play as you can (whether live or on film). It is helpful to keep a log book so you can keep track of your impressions while watching or soon after a performance.

* Try to act out as much of the play as you can, exploring different ways of saying key lines or working out how you would physically stage an encounter between two characters. Directing other people in a scene can reveal even more than acting in it.

* Engage actively with the play to help you think how to bring out your interpretation in performance and to consider alternative interpretations. You will also find you remember the play more clearly.

Always bear in mind that physical gestures in drama can change our view of a character and relationship. For example, our sense of the relationship between Hamlet and his father depends on how the 'love' that the Ghost mentions is shown in performance. In the 2008 Royal Shakespeare Company production, with David Tennant as Hamlet, there was a meaningful moment when the Ghost seems to hug him and Hamlet gave a gasp of love and grief. Through this non-verbal gesture, the audience were given another way of thinking about Hamlet's character.

While working through this book, you will have encountered many different critical views of Hamlet and constructed your own interpretations. As you work through the following section, consider how your interpretations relate to those offered by others. Keep a note of your findings, especially where you agree and disagree with a particular interpretation.

Hamlet and the question of delay

Debates about *Hamlet* have been going on for centuries. One of the biggest questions to preoccupy critics is why Hamlet delays taking action. It is a very hard question to answer, not least because Hamlet himself does not know: 'I do not know / Why yet I live to say this thing's to do' *(Act 4, Scene 4)*.

William Hazlitt's Hamlet

Traditional responses considered Hamlet's character, almost as if he were a real person. He was described by William Hazlitt (1778–1830), the English writer and critic, as a 'poet-philosopher', a very sensitive man and 'not a character marked by strength of will or even of passion, but by refinement of thought and sentiment [emotion or feeling]'. This Hamlet is very much a thinker, but paralysed by his thoughts. Hazlitt concluded that Hamlet 'is as little of the hero as a man can well be'. For him, Hamlet's delay is caused by being too emotional and thinking too much.

John Simm's Hamlet fails to take action while John Nettles's Claudius is praying, at the Crucible Theatre, Sheffield, 2010

A.C. Bradley's Hamlet

Another very influential Shakespeare critic, A.C. Bradley (1851–1935), took a similar approach. He argued that Hamlet's problem is his 'melancholy', or rapid and extreme changes of feeling and mood. According to Bradley, Hamlet's melancholy takes him over completely. When Hamlet says to Laertes, at Ophelia's grave in Act 5, Scene 1, that 'I loved you ever. But it is no matter', Bradley argues that Hamlet means that *nothing* matters any more. Bradley does not blame Hamlet for his delay or his depression. In fact, he sees Hamlet's goodness as the thing that destroys him, and the cause of his tragedy.

> ### Key quotation
>
> the native hue of resolution
> Is sicklied o'er with the pale cast of thought *(Hamlet, Act 3, Scene 1)*

Freudian interpretations

Later, the ideas of Sigmund Freud (1856–1939), the psychoanalyst, and his writings about the Oedipus complex, influenced interpretations of Hamlet's delay. Freud argued that the very young male child desires to replace the father in the mother's affections. As the child gets older, he grows out of this phase and the desire is repressed, excluding painful desires or fears from the conscious mind. However, if trauma occurred in childhood, the desire or fear it generated lurks in the adult's subconscious mind, influencing behaviour. (Psychoanalysts nowadays usually use the term 'unconscious'.)

Literary critics argued that Hamlet was driven by his subconscious sexual desire for his mother and tormented by his subconscious desire to kill his own father. According to the critic Ernest Jones, Claudius 'incorporates the deepest and most buried part' of Hamlet's personality: in killing Old Hamlet, Claudius has done what Hamlet's subconscious secretly wished to do. This means that Hamlet cannot kill Claudius 'without also killing himself', and he therefore delays.

Interpretations based so closely on Freud's theory of the Oedipus complex became less fashionable over the years, but elements of the Freudian reading continued to influence critics and productions. Critics point out that, whatever the reason for Hamlet's disgust with his mother, Shakespeare shows that Gertrude's sexual activity is at the heart of her son's psychological and emotional distress.

Joanne Pearce as Ophelia in the Royal Shakespeare Company's production at the Barbican Theatre, London in 1992

Others suggest that the Ghost's demand for revenge is a form of displacement activity. Because Hamlet's extreme feelings of sexual revulsion towards his mother are not socially acceptable, he replaces them with something more acceptable. Revenging his father would show him to be a good son and give his fury with his mother a more 'natural' and acceptable outlet.

Activity 1

Which, if any, of these interpretations of Hamlet's delay do you find most convincing? Give your reasons, providing evidence from the text. Alternatively, if none of them seems convincing to you, provide evidence from the text to justify your own view.

Queer readings

In recent years, critics have begun to challenge traditional representations and understandings of sexuality. 'Queer' theory, in particular, reveals the ways in which discussions of literature have centred on heterosexual norms. In the past, for example, a review of Hamlet's sexual identity or a discussion of love would have considered only his attitudes and behaviour towards women. Queer theorists ask us to focus on homosocial (male-male) relationships. Critics are not usually arguing that Horatio and Hamlet are involved in a romantic or sexual relationship, but highlighting Hamlet's 'love' for Horatio. Perhaps his homosocial bond with Horatio is stronger and more satisfying than his heterosexual attachment to Ophelia?

Feminist criticism

With all the focus on Hamlet, it was easy for critics to idealize, overlook or dismiss the female characters in the play. 'Poor Ophelia!' wrote Anna Jameson in 1832. The girl was simply 'too soft, too good, too fair' for the 'working-day world'. A.C. Bradley saw Ophelia as young and naïve, whilst Gertrude was dismissed as 'dull', 'shallow' and 'sensual'. The writer Rebecca West wrote of Gertrude that 'the whole play depends on her not noticing, and not understanding'.

Ophelia and madness

Feminist critics have encouraged new ways of thinking about Ophelia and her madness. As the American critic Elaine Showalter has explained, for 'many feminist theorists, the madwoman is a heroine, a powerful figure who rebels against the family and the social order'. In this reading of the play, Ophelia's madness paradoxically gives her power and allows her to express rebellion against the patriarchal order that has oppressed her. The rebellion against gender stereotypes is, however, achieved at the enormous cost of her madness and death.

Ophelia's innocence?

Just as Ophelia's madness has been reinterpreted as empowerment, her apparent innocence and naïvety have been questioned. Some productions have portrayed her as having a sexual relationship with Hamlet and even being pregnant by him. It could be argued that the explicit descriptions of sex in Ophelia's songs reveal that she is sexually experienced rather than repressed. Some critics go as far as to interpret Polonius in Act 1, Scene 3, when he tells Ophelia that she speaks 'like a green girl', as saying that she is in fact no such thing. Although she appears 'green' (innocent), and knows how to speak like an innocent girl, her own father knows she has been sexually active.

Activity 2

Find two reviews of recent productions of *Hamlet*, on stage or on film, and focus on what each reviewer writes about the characters and portrayals of Ophelia and Gertrude. Is there any evidence, in the production being reviewed, of any of the ideas about female characters outlined on page 94?

Historical criticism

In recent decades, critics have become more interested in trying to understand *Hamlet* as a product of a particular time and place – the very end of the 16th century in England. For example, Shakespeare can be seen to be exploring a world that has recently changed religion. As the critic Laurie Maguire explains, Catholic burial rites (which included lighting candles for the dead, wakes, ritual prayers and requiem masses) had been 'erased' by the Protestant Reformation in England. Maguire states that the 'Reformation swept away formal outlets for grief, leaving Protestants alone with their memories'. *Hamlet* therefore becomes a play about religious change and the impact this has on individuals.

Interiority

Hamlet begins with a question 'Who's there?' which is echoed just a few lines later: 'Who is there?' However, 'Who's there?' is not just a literal question, but the beginning of a complex exploration of psychological identity, of 'that within that passes show' (as Hamlet says in Act 1, Scene 2) which continues throughout the play. This exploration of **interiority** is often seen as one of the ways in which Shakespeare's drama was ground-breaking in his own time.

> **interiority** a character's thoughts and feelings. In drama, the character's inner life is usually revealed through soliloquies

The text(s) of *Hamlet*

Two very different versions of *Hamlet* were published in Shakespeare's lifetime. The first appeared in 1603 and is known as the First Quarto. You are studying a text derived from the longer and more literary Second Quarto (1604–5), which was a response to its dubious, possibly pirated, predecessor, being labelled 'Newly imprinted and enlarged to almost as much again as it was, according to the true and perfect copy'. Scholars are uncertain about the status of the First Quarto (was it an early draft? Was it a collaboration between Shakespeare and another playwright? Was it a less wordy touring version of the play?) but its existence reminds us that there is not one single, authorized version of *Hamlet*.

Take, for example, the most famous speech in *Hamlet*, 'To be or not to be…', which appears in Act 3, Scene 1 in the edition you are using. Not only are the words different in the First Quarto ('To be, or not to be – ay, there's the point…') but the speech comes earlier in the play.

The existence of the First Quarto encourages theatre companies to experiment with Shakespeare's text. However, when the director Lyndsey Turner had Benedict Cumberbatch speak 'To be or not to be…' at the very beginning of the play in 2015, there was an outcry. After a few weeks, the production returned to having the soliloquy in its familiar place. The truth is, however, that *Hamlet* has always been changing, since its first performance.

Political criticism

Rapid political and social change after the Second World War reinforced a political perspective on *Hamlet*. For the Polish critic and political activist Jan Kott, *Hamlet* was 'a drama of political crime'. The focus remained, however, on Hamlet, a young rebel 'deeply involved in politics, sarcastic, passionate and brutal' (*Shakespeare Our Contemporary, 1964*).

Critics have also argued that Gertrude (as an older woman) can be seen as a parallel to the ageing Queen Elizabeth I, who was in the final years of her reign when the play was written. Elizabeth had never married and had no obvious successor. However, this interpretation raises many questions. Is Shakespeare challenging or supporting the misogyny (prejudice against women) in the play? Is he celebrating the virgin Queen Elizabeth at the expense of the sexual Gertrude? Or perhaps the play suggests, as Hamlet does, that all women are the same; in which case, perhaps it points to the innate frailty and corruption of the real queen of England.

Politics and theatre in Shakespeare's time

More generally, critics have explored the ways in which drama was a political art form during Shakespeare's lifetime.

New historicist critics, who became influential in the 1980s, tried to show the dynamic relation between what had traditionally been seen as (literary) text and (historical) context. They argued that literary works were shaped by historical events, but also that literature shaped society. Critics such as Stephen Greenblatt argued that in Shakespeare's time, public ceremonial was closely connected with statecraft, with the monarch consolidating power through displays of political theatre.

It could be argued that theatre also supported the status quo. King James I became the patron of Shakespeare's theatre company and Shakespeare's plays were regularly performed at court. The playwright Thomas Heywood (1570–1641) wrote that plays were written and performed to teach 'subjects obedience to their king'. The stage could be compared to the scaffold, where the crowd would enjoy the spectacle of public executions unfolding like theatre whilst being shown that evil was punished.

On the other hand, Heywood wrote these words in a work called *An Apology for Actors* in which the acting profession is defended from the charge that plays encouraged disobedience and even rebellion. Theatre, it was argued in Shakespeare's time, could help people to understand the workings of power and therefore to question the authorities and hierarchies that kept people in their place.

Each generation makes *Hamlet* in its own image. Each generation responds to *Hamlet* in its own way. In our own time, for example, the writer Margaret Atwood has responded to the play with a short story called 'Gertrude Talks Back'. Atwood offers a modern take on Gertrude's character, written in the form of a monologue, and with a wickedly funny punchline.

Writing about critical views

When you bring your critical reading into an essay, do try to name the critic and (especially if the critic was writing many years ago) indicate roughly when the interpretation was offered. But, most importantly, always try to show how a critical view relates to your own interpretation of the text. The critic might confirm, complicate and/or contradict your interpretation. All these are valid uses of critical views.

Exam skills

Preparing for your assessment

Make sure you know the structure of the exam paper you will be taking so that the format becomes completely familiar. You need to know:

- if you will have a choice of questions
- whether to expect a question in two or more parts
- how the mark scheme works
- how many marks you can gain for each question.

Timing

Think carefully how you are going to organize the time available in the exam. Some calculations are straightforward and work for everyone. For example, if you have two hours and two questions to answer, you have about an hour for each question.

Remember to factor in time for planning at the start and checking your work at the end. Although everyone is different, many students need about five minutes for planning and about five minutes for checking.

You should always use the full time allocated for your exam. If you finish early, you have probably not written enough. If that happens, it is perfectly acceptable to add an extra paragraph, even if it should go in the middle of your essay, as long as you mark where it goes clearly, so the examiner can understand what you are doing.

Focusing on the question

Before you begin your assessment:

- read the question carefully
- underline the key words.

Make sure you do not rush into writing without properly focusing on the specific question. You will lose marks if you make basic errors, such as answering only one part of a two-part question or writing about the wrong character or theme. Even if you think you have answered a similar question before, make sure you identify exactly what is being asked of you, as the question might be slightly different.

Answering extract–based questions

If you are answering an extract-based question, remember that you are being asked to offer a close reading of the extract. This involves picking out key words, phrases and literary devices, and analysing them with insight. The extract will have been chosen because there is plenty to say about it.

As you read through the extract, underline key words or phrases, and annotate them. This will help you to focus on details of language.

Look out for:

- the language that is used, especially imagery, similes and metaphors
- the structure (for example, how the extract begins and ends)
- the form (for example, if it is in blank verse or prose)
- whether the audience learns anything new from the extract
- lines or actions that could be interpreted in different ways
- opportunities to display any relevant understanding about context
- how the extract fits into the whole play in terms of plot and genre.

Remember the following points when answering extract-based questions:

- You are expected to refer to the extract in detail, using appropriate quotations.
- Cover the whole extract in your answer: spending 90% of your essay on the first few lines is never a good approach.
- Make connections between the extract and the rest of the play, but ensure that quotations and references from the rest of the play are relevant to the question.
- When writing about an extract, it is still really important to read the question carefully.

Remember that drama is written to be performed on stage in front of an audience. Therefore, when analysing a passage from *Hamlet*, you need to think and write about the play *in performance*. The words on the page are only half the story: think 'page to stage' and it will keep you focused. (It will help if you have seen at least one performance of *Hamlet*, live or recorded, and if you have acted out some parts of the play yourself.)

Tips for assessment

If appropriate to the question, show awareness of different critical approaches to the extract. For example, you could suggest how a feminist critic or a Freudian critic might analyse it.

Understanding the question

Understanding command words

Your first step should be to work out what precisely is being asked. You can do this by focusing on the key instructions in the question. Below are some examples of key instructions, followed by a typical essay-style question and an explanation of what it requires:

How does the author...? or Show how...

You need to explain the techniques the author uses to create a specific effect. The word 'how' is the key instruction, asking you to analyse Shakespeare's way of writing. It is a way of reminding you that the characters are not real people but constructed by Shakespeare. For example:

> How does Shakespeare present death in *Hamlet*?

You need to consider the different dramatic ways Shakespeare presents the theme of death. You need to write about the language Shakespeare uses, including imagery and symbols, as well as how particular deaths are staged, when they occur in the play and their significance to its overall effects. You could also consider Shakespeare's use of comedy to explore the subject of death, as in the graveyard scene.

Explore...

This means look at all the different aspects of something, but it also encourages you to analyse rather than simply describe what a character says or does. For example:

> Explore how Shakespeare represents madness.

You should consider Shakespeare's representation of madness from different angles throughout the play. Your exploration must be more than a list. For the highest marks, it will involve showing why madness is important to the play as a whole and considering different critical interpretations of the madness in the play.

In what ways...?

These key words ask you to look at the different sides to something, and is therefore similar to 'explore'. For example:

> In what ways is Claudius significant to *Hamlet*?

You must consider more than one way that Claudius is important to the play. You could, for example, start by arguing that he is significant because he is the villain, and connect this with the genre of revenge tragedy, in which villains are often more active than the hero. Additional considerations might include how he functions as a mirror to other characters (for example, Old Hamlet) or what his actions in the final scene reveal about him. For the highest marks, you should show awareness of different critical assessments of Claudius, including the argument that Shakespeare creates a character who is an effective and capable leader, and how that impacts on the audience's view of Hamlet.

What role...?

You need to write not just about the character and how Shakespeare creates the character, but also about the character's function in the play. (Above, in the question about Claudius, the word 'significant' asks you to do the same thing.) For example:

> What role does Fortinbras play in *Hamlet*?

To answer this question, you must write about the character of Fortinbras but, more importantly, consider why he is in the play at all. One way of approaching this is to imagine the play without the character. What would be missing? Always bear in mind *how* Shakespeare makes a character significant to the play. It may not simply be a question of how many lines the character has, but where those lines come in the timeline of the play or their actions.

How far...? Do you agree...? To what extent...?

All these phrases ask you to make a value judgement about an aspect of the play. You need to create an argument in which you weigh up the evidence for or against. For example:

> To what extent are women represented as victims in *Hamlet*?

You need to write about how women are represented as victims in the play, but also to offer alternative understandings of their characters and roles. Although your focus should be on the female characters in the play, you could also bring in your understanding of women's lives in Shakespeare's time and/or even contrast the female characters with the male characters. Make sure you consider a range of ideas, but always come back to the original question and say whether you agree or disagree.

Looking at other key words

Look at the question below, where the key words and phrases have been underlined and explained.

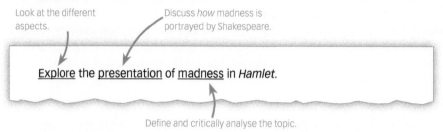

Look at the different aspects.

Discuss *how* madness is portrayed by Shakespeare.

Explore the presentation of madness in *Hamlet*.

Define and critically analyse the topic.

You are being asked to do a number of things in this question. Your absolute priority is to show *how* Shakespeare presents madness, but that could also encompass:

- how Shakespeare presents (or contrasts) the madness of Ophelia and of Hamlet, which you can relate to his use of doubling, foils or parallels in the play
- how Shakespeare makes madness important to the play as a whole, which you can relate to the genre of tragedy, as a movement from order to disorder (with order re-established at the end)
- how Shakespeare makes it difficult for us to assess whether Hamlet's madness is real and why that uncertainty is important to the play as a whole
- how Ophelia's madness has been performed, how those performance choices are important to the play as a whole, and/or how the representation of Ophelia's madness has been interpreted by feminist critics.

Activity 1

a) Copy the following question and highlight or underline the key words and phrases.

b) Describe in your own words what you are being asked to do.

Show how Horatio is important to the play as a whole.

Planning your answer

Thinking about and planning your answer will help you to:

- structure it logically
- focus correctly on all aspects of the question
- avoid missing out crucial points
- include a good range of quotations and literary terminology.

You should take a few minutes to plan your answer before you start writing. Some students might simply put together a brief checklist of information needed for each section of the essay. This will stop you repeating yourself or wandering off topic. It will also give you confidence to keep going if you get stuck during the exam.

Practise by planning answers to a variety of questions. However, do not learn your practice answers by heart, hoping that you can use them in the actual exam. The skill you are developing is to be able to *think* and be creative under exam conditions, so that you can respond to the specific question that is being asked.

Spider diagrams

You could use a spider diagram to plan your answer. You need to make sure that your plan remains focused on the key words of the question.

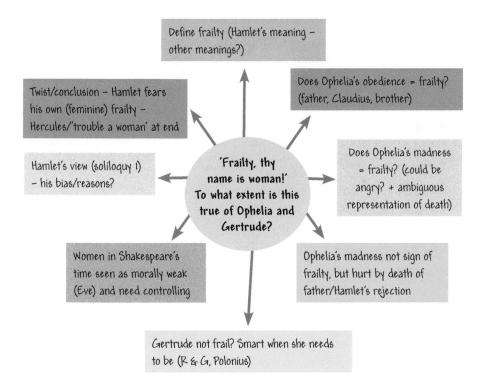

Activity 2

Use a spider diagram to plan an answer to each of the following questions.

- How is revenge presented in *Hamlet*?
- In what ways is Polonius significant to *Hamlet*?

Paragraphs

You might choose to plan your essay by creating paragraph headings. For example:

'Frailty, thy name is woman.' To what extent is this true of Ophelia and Gertrude?

Paragraph 1 Introduction: 'frailty': Hamlet's first soliloquy, what he means/his bias. What else can frailty mean?

Paragraph 2 Ophelia's obedience to father, king, brother = frailty?

Paragraph 3 Ophelia's madness = frailty?

Paragraph 4 Not frail – hurt by death of father/Hamlet's rejection

Paragraph 5 Questions about Ophelia's death (relate to Hamlet's thoughts on suicide/death) – questions raised by play about heroism/strength ('suffer the slings and arrows' or 'take arms')

Paragraph 6 Gertrude: traditional view = she's unintelligent, passive, unimportant but she is quite smart/quick (R & G, Polonius); relationship with Claudius

Paragraph 7 Context: women in Shakespeare's time seen as morally weak (Eve) and need controlling

Paragraph 8 Conclusion: this is Hamlet's view; he is fearful of his own (feminine) frailty: Hercules/'trouble a woman' at end.

Activity 3

Explore which approach to planning an essay works best for you.

a) Prepare a spider diagram to plan an essay for one or more of the essay questions below.

b) Then plan these essays using a paragraph plan.

c) Highlight what you think are the most important points in each plan.

To what extent do you think Ophelia is important to *Hamlet*?

Explore the presentation of violence in the play.

How does Shakespeare use different settings in *Hamlet*?

Writing your answer

It may help to use some of the wording from the original question in your introductory paragraph, at appropriate points throughout your essay and especially in the final paragraph. This will ensure that you stay on topic and answer the question that has been set.

Avoid starting your essay with 'In this essay I am going to…'. Instead, launch straight into it. Some students find it helpful to start by stating a strong, perhaps even controversial, idea in their opening paragraph. This launches you straight into your argument because you will then have to prove your idea to be valid.

Your answer should show your knowledge and understanding of:

- what the author is saying
- how the author is saying it
- how the context influences or illuminates the content of the play.

You also need to help the examiner follow your thinking, so signpost your argument with sentence starters such as: However, …; In contrast, …; Moreover, …; Ironically, …; Similarly, …. Using these types of words also encourages you to link different perspectives, and to avoid simply telling the story or writing a list of points.

Remember to use the correct tone and style in your writing. One way of making sure you get this right is to read some Shakespeare criticism. Read at least one of the following:

- the introduction to an edition of *Hamlet*
- the programme for a production of the play
- one of the more accessible books of Shakespeare criticism available (see the reading list on page 119).

Also, remember that the examiner has read the text you are writing about and knows it extremely well, so there is absolutely no need to explain the plot or who the characters are!

What to avoid when writing your answer

- Do not write a long introduction showing what you know about Shakespeare's life or his other plays. Only refer to his life or other plays briefly and only if it is relevant to the point you are making about *Hamlet*.

- Do not write long paragraphs about the historical or social context. Even if this information is relevant to your understanding of *Hamlet*, you need to cover it briefly and then come back quickly to the specific question and your analysis of the play text.

- Do not try to write everything you know about the text. You are being assessed on your ability to shape what you know into an essay that answers the question.

- Ideally, your essay will end with a short conclusion, drawing your ideas together. However, don't simply repeat your ideas but add something new as well.

Tips for assessment

The most common mistake made by students is simply to retell the plot or to describe a character or event. To avoid this, make sure that every paragraph of your essay includes ideas, evidence and analysis, and is directly relevant to the question.

Using quotations

You must support your ideas and interpretations with evidence, often in the form of quotations, from the text. The best way to do this is by using PEA:

- make a **Point**
- provide **Evidence** that is relevant to your point
- **Analyse** the evidence and explain why it is relevant to your point.

You could use phrases such as:

- This makes it clear to the audience that…
- This shows that…
- Shakespeare is showing us that…

Hamlet is a complex play full of moments when it is difficult for the audience to be certain about what is happening. To make this point, you might also begin, 'Here Shakespeare makes it hard to decide whether…'.

Supporting your ideas in this way means you will need to memorize some quotations. Even if you are doing an extract-based question, you may want to refer to another part of the play in a precise way. It is best to select short passages that are likely to be relevant to a variety of questions, rather than trying to memorize long sections of the text.

When you use a short quotation, it should be embedded into your writing in a grammatically correct way. Using quotations effectively as part of your sentences (rather than simply adding them onto the end) is a skill you can practise. This is a great way to show that you know the text well, without having to learn or write out long quotations.

Spelling, punctuation and grammar

It is important that you use spelling, punctuation and grammar accurately. This will make a good impression but, more importantly, will help the examiner understand the points you want to make. However brilliant your point is, if the examiner cannot understand it, you will not gain marks for it.

Always allow time to check your work. Practise checking for the following mistakes:

- misspelling the title of the text or the names of its author or characters
- writing over-long paragraphs. If in doubt, divide up a long paragraph
- forgetting to use common punctuation such as commas
- misusing capital letters
- using words from social media or slang
- leaving out words.

Your work will be even stronger if you do the following:

- vary the opening of your sentences
- avoid over-use of the word 'I'
- use linking phrases such as 'in contrast', 'ironically' or 'initially'
- use phrases such as 'significantly' or 'most importantly' to indicate when you are making your most important points
- clearly signpost your argument, through words and phrases such as: However...; An alternative way of understanding this scene is...; This view is complicated by...; This is confirmed by...; In conclusion....

Activity 4

a) Check that you know how to spell the main characters' names. Test yourself by writing them all out.

b) Then do the same with:

- names of the minor characters (for example, Rosencrantz and Guildenstern)
- any other names and proper nouns from the play (for example, Wittenberg and Elsinore)
- tricky critical or literary terms (for example, peripeteia).

Sample questions

You should get as much practice as possible in answering a range of different essay questions. You will find examples of questions throughout this Skills and Practice chapter. Some of them have example answers provided and others appear in the activities. In addition, the examples below will be useful for planning and writing answers in full.

1
Show how Shakespeare makes fathers and fatherhood important to the tragedy in *Hamlet*. Where relevant, you should refer to contextual factors you have explored in your critical reading.

2
Do you agree that Shakespeare shows Laertes to be a more successful revenge hero than Hamlet?

3
At the start of the play, the Ghost asks Hamlet to revenge his 'foul and most unnatural murder'. At the end, Horatio speaks of 'unnatural acts'. Explore Shakespeare's representation of the idea of the 'unnatural' in *Hamlet*.

4
Show how Shakespeare mixes comedy with tragedy in *Hamlet* and explore the dramatic effect of this mixture.

5
Explore the ways in which Shakespeare's use of doubling (in plot, character and language) contributes to the complexity of the play.

6
In one of Shakespeare's sources, Gertrude is described as a 'brute beast'. Does Shakespeare present her in this way? Your answer should consider different interpretations of the play.

7
In what ways can *Hamlet* be seen as an exploration of heroism? Remember to include relevant analaysis of Shakespeare's dramatic methods.

8

The performance of 'The Mousetrap' has been described as the 'principle turning point' in *Hamlet*. Do you agree?

9

'There's such divinity doth hedge a king', says Claudius, in Act 4, Scene 5. Explore the representation of divinity and/or kingship in *Hamlet*. Your answer should refer to relevant contextual factors and ideas from your critical reading.

10

In what ways, and to what extent, is order restored at the end of *Hamlet*? Remember to include relevant analysis of Shakespeare's dramatic methods in your answer.

11

How does Shakespeare represent suicide in *Hamlet*? Your answer should make reference to different interpretations.

12

'I loved Ophelia', says *Hamlet* in Act 5, Scene 1. Do you agree that he did? To what extent is your answer important to an understanding of the play as a whole?

Sample answers

Sample answer 1

'The whole play depends on Gertrude not noticing and not understanding'.
Do you agree with this assessment of Gertrude's role in *Hamlet*?

Gertrude is Hamlet's mother and she does notice that he is depressed at
the beginning of the play. Maybe she understands why he is depressed,
because she talks about her 'hasty marriage' and knows that Hamlet is
still missing his father. But Gertrude does not really understand Hamlet's
behaviour, which is why she agrees that his school friends should be used
to try to find out what is wrong with him.

A scene in which Gertrude does not notice or understand what is
happening is the closet scene. Gertrude does not see the Ghost and
therefore thinks that Hamlet is mad. In the final scene of the play,
Gertrude doesn't understand what is happening. She doesn't know
that Claudius has poisoned the wine. Gertrude can be seen as weak.
For example, when the news comes that Ophelia is mad, she doesn't
want to see her. Some productions show Gertrude to be an alcoholic.
This would provide a reason for her not noticing and not understanding.
She is trying to block life out with drink.

However, there are some moments when Gertrude is assertive. She corrects
her husband when he gets names wrong and she tries to make Polonius
hurry up, saying 'more matter with less art'. When she is watching the
play, she comments that 'the lady doth protest too much'. She is actually
quite sharp and intelligent.

Perhaps one of the reasons the audience thinks Gertrude does not notice
or understand much is that Shakespeare does not give her many lines or
a soliloquy. This means the audience does not know the character well or
hear her private thoughts.

Hamlet's opinion of his mother is therefore very powerful on the audience.
He is full of anger towards her and women in general: 'Frailty thy name
is woman!' Hamlet's attitude to his mother is very typical of the time in
which the play was written. Women were supposed to be silent, chaste and
obedient. Gertrude is quite silent and obedient but, according to Hamlet,
she is not chaste because she is having sex with Claudius, which disgusts
him because she shouldn't be having sex in 'incestuous sheets'.

No need to state obvious
facts about characters.

Good use of embedded
quotation.

Continues to
refer to Gertrude
as a real person,
instead of referring
to Shakespeare's
techniques.

Good focus using the
key words from the
question.

Shows knowledge of the
shape of the play.

Paragraph needs
evidence and analysis.

Attempts to bring in
performance, but would
be better with evidence.

Uses evidence well to
back up evaluations of
Gertrude's character.

Identifies Gertrude as a
character within a play.

Shows good awareness
of the audience.

Links context to
the play well.

Embeds quotation
effectively.

Returns to the question and moves the argument along well.

Avoid using slang.

Shows awareness of sources but better if more precise.

So although Gertrude is important because of things she doesn't do (like notice or understand what's going on), she is more important to the play because of what she does do, which is having sex with Claudius. It is this that freaks out Hamlet. Shakespeare's sources focused on this side to Gertrude's character. She was called a 'brute beast'. Some productions of Hamlet make the relationship between Hamlet and his mother sexual. For example, David Tennant stood 'astride' Gertrude on her bed.

Gertrude can be compared to Ophelia. Not noticing and not understanding is something that Ophelia has to do in the play. When Hamlet makes obscene jokes during 'The Mousetrap', Ophelia cannot respond or show that she understands his words about 'country matters'. So, perhaps not noticing and not understanding is something women have to do to survive in the world of Elsinore.

Makes a thoughtful point, with evidence, closely linked to the question.

Refers to Gertrude as a dramatic creation.

Makes an excellent reference to genre.

Shows awareness of Shakespeare's dramatic methods.

Gertrude is not a well-developed character. She is not a protagonist. This is partly because she conforms to ideas about women of the time (e.g. she is not as intelligent as the male characters) but also because in tragedy the heroes were usually male. However, although it is possible to understand her weakness and lack of intelligence, Shakespeare does not make it important to the play. The ending of Hamlet does not 'depend' on it. This is shown in the lack of attention paid to Gertrude's death at the end of the play. She doesn't really matter. The struggle going on between Hamlet and Claudius is much more important to the play.

This essay is at its strongest when the candidate remembers to write about Gertrude as a character created by Shakespeare, rather than as a real person. It is a thoughtful, intelligent essay, but many of the points sound superficial. If they had been supported by quotations and references, which had been analysed, the essay would be very good indeed.

Activity 5

Using the advice given above and what you know about *Hamlet*, rewrite and improve sample answer 1.

Sample answer 2

> In what ways is theatre important to *Hamlet*?

Hamlet explores the power and significance of theatre, and of performance, upon audiences. The language of theatre runs through every scene, with the repetition of words such as 'play', 'act', 'show', 'perform' and 'part'. The importance of theatre is demonstrated by the fact that Shakespeare slows down what his audience would have expected to be a fast-paced, action-filled revenge tragedy with long discussions about theatre, and long speeches from drama.

Immediately focuses on language.

Clearly refers to genre and links to the question.

The play as a whole explores the idea of acting, so that by the end we see many of the characters as actors and are uncertain of what is really going on behind the mask. Hamlet himself puts on 'an antic disposition', suggesting he can put off the part whenever he wants. But one of the most interesting questions raised by the play is whether acting as a madman does in fact make him mad.

First of many short, relevant embedded quotations.

Hamlet's 'delight' in the visiting players' intense performance quickly turns to disgust with himself. He sees it as 'monstrous' that the actor can in a 'fiction, in a dream of passion' force tears from his eyes – and 'all for nothing!' Out of this moment comes Hamlet's plan to use theatre to test the reliability of the Ghost. Audiences in Shakespeare's time would have seen echoes of the most famous revenge tragedy of the era, 'The Spanish Tragedy', which has a play within a play. But Shakespeare has Hamlet use the play in a completely different way. In 'The Spanish Tragedy' the play is a way to achieve revenge. In Hamlet, 'The Mousetrap' is an attempt to find out if revenge is necessary.

Better to follow up with a reference and an opinion.

Shows relevant, detailed knowledge of the play.

Excellent use of context, clearly linked to discussion of Hamlet.

Clearly signposts an interesting shift in argument.

There is, however, something ironic in Hamlet's decision to use theatre to test the reality of the Ghost. In Shakespeare's time, people saw a connection between the Devil and theatre. The Ghost might be an illusion (a piece of demonic theatricality, according to the critic Stephen Greenblatt) created by the Devil in order to 'abuse' Hamlet. Hamlet claims to be 'prompted' to his 'revenge by heaven and hell', which, typically for the play, simply offers the audiences alternatives without resolving the issue.

Uses critical view well to make the point more precise.

Sets the argument about theatre in wider context of the difficulty of interpreting *Hamlet*.

There is another way in which Shakespeare makes the audience think about theatre and acting. Hamlet is a famous example of metatheatre, theatre about theatre. It is partly the references to Shakespeare's own London theatre world (Hamlet asks about the rise of boy actors, 'little

Moves the essay on. Could this have been linked to previous points?

Gives a definition.

Gives two examples of *Hamlet* as metatheatre.

eyases', the new competitors to Shakespeare's own King's Men at the Globe), and partly the experience of watching Hamlet watching Claudius watching 'The Mousetrap'. The audience is constantly reminded that they are watching theatre. Indeed, the whole play appears preoccupied with playing, stages, acting and fictions. This all encourages the audience to see life as essentially theatrical, as Shakespeare has another of his melancholic characters, Jacques in As You Like It, say: 'All the world's a stage, and all the men and women merely players'.

Elegant and relevant use of context.

The Players' scenes allow Shakespeare to explore the theme of seeming further. Hamlet is extremely disturbed that the actor can cry real tears and move his audience. In contrast, Hamlet not only cannot express his own feelings, but he cannot communicate those feelings to others. He does indeed have 'that within which passeth show', as he says to his mother in his opening scene.

Focuses on one soliloquy but makes a confident, elegant link to earlier in the play.

Shakespeare forces the audience to think about acting and consider all the other characters who 'act' in this play. Characters like Rosencrantz and Guildenstern are acting when they are with Hamlet, pretending that Claudius has not sent them to 'play' upon Hamlet. Ophelia is forced into a performance in the nunnery scene. In a play obsessed with seeming, and the difficulty of establishing truth, Horatio is one of the few characters who does not put on a part. He just stays himself: perhaps this is one of the reasons he is not 'passion's slave'.

Refocuses to consider characters.

Claudius is the most obvious example of a character who performs a part successfully on the political stage. In the opening court scene, we see him in confident command of his onstage audience, introducing, commanding and, in the case of Fortinbras ('So much for him'), dismissing other characters. Claudius, it can be argued, is a master of political theatre.

Makes an excellent point well.

It is significant that at the end of the play, another master of political – or perhaps military – theatre takes over in Denmark: Fortinbras who orders his soldiers to take Hamlet's body 'like a soldier to the stage'. (It was actually Horatio's idea that Hamlet should be placed 'high on a stage', revealing that he is worried about the effect of the carnage on 'men's minds'. Earlier Horatio had been concerned that Ophelia's madness would 'strew dangerous conjectures in ill-breeding minds'.) Shakespeare appears to be suggesting that political stability will be ensured only if the deaths are staged correctly. One kind of theatre – the 'trappings' that Hamlet rejects at the beginning of the play, 'the inexplicable dumb-shows and noise' that he despises – replaces another, the subtle exploration of Hamlet's psychology through soliloquy and dialogue.

The content is well analysed and integrated, leading to a powerful closing argument about theatre and politics.

This is an exceptionally strong essay, showing a detailed knowledge of the text and offering a variety of answers to the question. Although the candidate does not mention specific performances, the sense of a play as a play is very clear.

Sample answer 3

Read the extract from Act 3, Scene 4, from Hamlet's line 'Not this, by no means…' to the end of the scene.

Starting with the extract, how does Shakespeare explore the idea of madness in the play? Write about:

- how Shakespeare presents madness in this extract
- how Shakespeare presents madness in the play as a whole.

In this extract, Shakespeare makes it hard for the reader to work out whether Hamlet is mad. Hamlet is worried because he believes his mother will tell Claudius that he is 'not in madness'. This suggests that Hamlet is still hoping that the antic disposition he put on as an act at the beginning of the play will protect him from being punished for the killing of Polonius.

Shows awareness of the text as a literary work.

Relates the extract to another part of the play, but quotation marks are needed.

Hamlet fears that Claudius will 'pinch wanton' on Gertrude's cheek, 'call you his mouse', and get her to reveal everything Hamlet has said in their discussion in the closet scene.

Slips into recounting the extract rather than analysing it.

The problem is that while Hamlet is telling Gertrude that he is sane, his own use of language suggests that he is not in control. His violent anger and disgust with the 'wanton' activities of his mother and Claudius emerge in his language: 'reechy kisses', 'damn'd fingers' and 'bloat king'. His use of animal imagery shows that he sees their sexual life as animalistic or bestial. Shakespeare makes us question Hamlet's balance of mind because of the intensity of his language. This makes Gertrude's belief that the Ghost, which she can't see, is 'the very coinage' of Hamlet's brain, a product of 'ecstasy' (madness), more understandable. Earlier, Ophelia had explained Hamlet's behaviour towards her as 'ecstasy'.

Excellent refocus on analysis and language.

Uses PEA very well in this paragraph.

Shows knowledge of the play, but is not so relevant.

Hamlet reminds his mother that he is being sent to England. He reveals that he does not trust Rosencrantz and Guildenstern. 'Adders fang'd' is another animal image. Hamlet is confident that he will be able to revenge himself on them: 'For 'tis the sport to have the enginer / Hoist with his own petard'. This is the second time Hamlet seems to be enjoying the thought of revenge. Just before talking with this mother, he fantasizes about killing Claudius when he is 'in th'incestuous pleasure of his bed' or another sinful act. Hamlet will 'trip him that his heels may kick at heaven.'

Connects the extract with the rest of the play well but wanders away from the topic of madness.

This is a new, vindictive Hamlet, who sees revenge as 'sport' and we hear the same voice in his desire to 'blow them (Rosencrantz and Guildenstern) to the moon'. Hamlet's reference to Polonius as 'the guts' shows another, unattractive side to his personality and in performance this simply adds to one of the things that is shocking about this scene, in that Hamlet and Gertrude continue talking despite there being a dead body lying on stage. The extract as a whole raises serious questions about Hamlet's sanity.

I would argue that Hamlet begins the play suffering from what we would call depression and intensely mourning his father. But he is also angry with his mother and obsessed with her marriage to Claudius: 'O most wicked speed! To post / With such dexterity to incestuous sheets.' (In the extract, Hamlet focuses on the king and his mother in 'bed', and Claudius getting the truth from Gertrude with 'reechy kisses').

The killing of Polonius, which occurs in this scene, leads to the real madness of Ophelia: 'divided from herself and her fair judgement'. Shakespeare asks us to compare Hamlet's fake 'antic disposition' (and talk of suicide) with Ophelia's real madness (and actual suicide). The comparison suggests that Hamlet is not mad. However, in the final scene, Hamlet himself says he was mad. Anything he has done that is wrong he proclaims was 'madness'. When Hamlet is 'not himself', he is not responsible for his behaviour. 'His madness is poor Hamlet's enemy'.

But in the extract here, Hamlet claims to be 'mad in craft'. This is another example of a way in which Shakespeare complicates his revenge tragedy, forcing the audience to think about what is true and what is acting.

Shows excellent awareness of performance.

Good idea to come back, directly, to the question.

Keeps the extract in focus, with good use of brackets.

Needs a clearer link to avoid apparent jump into new material and argument.

Would be better embedded into the sentence, not just at the end.

Better to analyse these quotations and not to use a standalone quotation.

Attempts to bring in genre, but it is quite late to bring in such a new idea.

This is quite a strong essay, especially when it analyses, rather than describes, the text. There is a good knowledge of the text, with clear connections made between the extract and the rest of the play. Although there seem to be plenty of quotations and references, they are not always integrated into the discussion or evaluated.

Sample answer 4

> Read the extract from Act 1, Scene 2, from the beginning of the scene up to Claudius's line, 'What woulds't thou have, Laertes?'
>
> Explore the ways in which Shakespeare presents the character of Claudius in this extract, and relate this extract to the representation of Claudius in the play as a whole.

This is the second scene in 'Hamlet'. It comes after the scene on the battlements and is brightly lit after the darkness. Claudius makes a long speech, saying he has married Gertrude ('our sometime sister') very soon after the death of the old king. Shakespeare makes Claudius sound really confident. One production showed Claudius giving this speech as a kind of press conference, which brings out his ability to speak well and to give people what they want. His speech is well structured and he pauses between each section: 'For all, our thanks. Now follows…'. Claudius calls Old Norway 'impotent'. The word means powerless, but it also has a sexual meaning. This may be a way for Claudius to contrast himself with old Norway and to show that he is powerful sexually and politically.

Not relevant to the question.

Refers to Claudius as a character rather than as a real person.

Shows awareness of the play in performance, but could be more precise about the production.

Focuses on language well, with analysis and interpretation.

We know from the stage directions that Gertrude is on stage with Claudius and she usually stands or sits next to him when he gives his long speech. She is like a trophy wife, but maybe she looks up at him adoringly.

Good awareness of silent characters but the point about performance could perhaps be more precise.

After talking about his marriage to Gertrude, Claudius turns to dealing with young Fortinbras. He sets out what he is going to do about Fortinbras and sends Voltemand and Cornelius to Norway to sort things out. This shows that Claudius expects to be obeyed.

Offers sensible analysis but there is no need to recount the story.

Claudius then turns to Laertes, repeating his name twice. This might be because Laertes is shy about coming forward. In one production it is made clear that Hamlet, who is more important than Laertes because he is the prince, is expecting Claudius to talk to him, and the king's decision to deal with Laertes first is a way to humiliate Hamlet in public.

Offers good critical analysis but could be more precise about the production.

Claudius remains in control throughout the play. He deals with problems quickly. For example, he decides to send Hamlet to England and makes sure someone guards Ophelia when she is mad. When Laertes bursts in and threatens him, Claudius deals with him too.

Makes a sudden jump without effective linking words.

Includes useful references.

Shakespeare only gives one scene in which the audience see the private, secret Claudius. In his soliloquy, in which he tries to pray but can't, Claudius tells the audience that his 'offence is rank, it smells to heaven'.

Summarizes a key scene well, with some quotation.

Having given two perspectives on Claudius (commander, guilty murderer), draws a conclusion from them before moving on.

> He knows what he has done but cannot 'repent' because that would mean giving up everything he has gained from killing his brother.

> Hamlet is right to say that 'one may smile, and smile, and be a villain' because this is true of Claudius. In the final scene, Claudius has a chance to do something good. He could have stopped Gertrude drinking the poisoned wine but he doesn't. Not only that, he lies about it. He knows that she is poisoned, but he says 'She swoons to see them bleed'. He deserves to die.

Loses sight of the play as a play and Shakespeare's choices.

> Some people have argued that, because Hamlet has so many problems, Claudius is actually the true hero of the play. However, being powerful and successful, as shown in the extract, does not make him the hero, but it does make him an interesting villain.

Makes a strong argument about the character in relation to the play as a whole. It would be even stronger if knowledge of revenge tragedy was included.

This essay may have a straightforward style and seem a bit mechanical but it stays focused on the question. The candidate succeeds in making a series of points about the language in the extract and ends with a clear if quite simple argument about Claudius's role as villain, which shows knowledge of the play as a whole.

Glossary and Further reading

allusion   reference

ambiguous   open to more than one interpretation

aside   a kind of stage whisper, a behind-the-hand comment made to the audience, that other characters cannot hear

back story   the history of what has already happened

blank verse   unrhymed verse; the five beats in each line are known as iambic pentameter

caesura   a break or pause in a line of poetry

catharsis   a Greek word meaning cleansing or purification

climax   the point in a literary work in which the tension reaches its highest point

closet   bedroom or private room

denouement   resolution of the conflicts represented in a literary work

doubling   in the theatre, when one actor plays two parts (e.g. in *Hamlet*, the actor playing the Ghost often also plays Claudius); in literary criticism, the many different kinds of dualism or doubleness, whether in plot, character or language

dramatic irony   when the audience knows more than the character

eloquence   the ability to use language well and persuasively

enigmatic   difficult to understand, mysterious

exposition   introduction of events, settings and characters to the audience

falling action   sequence of events after the climax but before the resolution

foil   a character who contrasts and parallels the main character in a play or story

gendered language   language that identifies something as either masculine or feminine

hamartia   a tragic flaw in a character

iambic beat   rhythm in which the first syllable is unstressed and the second is stressed/emphasized, e.g. the word 'because' is always an iamb, with stress on the second syllable

imagery   figurative (non-literal) language, especially metaphors and similes

interiority   a character's thoughts and feelings. In drama, the character's inner life is usually revealed through soliloquies

melancholy   sad or depressed; in Shakespeare's time, mental disturbance ranging from sadness to insanity

metaphor   when a person or thing is described by comparison with someone or something else without using words such as 'like' or 'as', e.g. 'you are a rock'

metre   the rhythm of a line of poetry

monosyllable   a word of one syllable

patriarchy   a way of organizing life (political, religious, social or personal) so that men have power, including over women, justified in Shakespeare's time by the Bible

peripeteia   a sudden change in events or reversal of fortunes

prose   writing that is not poetry and usually written in ordinary language without obviously rhythmical structure

protagonist   the central character or leading figure in a story

pun   a play on words

register   the form of a language used by a social group or in a particular social setting (e.g. slang)

revenge tragedy   a form of drama that is sensational and extremely violent. It was popular in Shakespeare's time and often known as 'tragedy of blood'

rhyming couplet   a pair of lines in poetry that rhyme

rising action   series of incidents that create tension and interest for the audience

satirize   ridicule, condemn

simile   when a person or thing is described by comparison with someone or something else, using words such as 'like' or 'as', e.g. 'you are like a rock'

soliloquy   speech by an actor made when he or she is alone on stage, generally reflecting on thoughts and feelings

spondee   two stressed syllables together

stage direction   part of a play script that indicates setting, movement, physical action

subplot   a secondary plot (storyline) that runs alongside and supports the main plot

subtext   the implicit or underlying meaning

symbolism   the use of concrete objects in language to represent abstract ideas or concepts

tragedy   a serious work (usually a play) in which the main character becomes involved in conflict with disastrous results and the course of events is usually presented as inevitable

tragic irony   when the audience knows more than the character and there is a tragic outcome

trochee   a strong syllable, followed by a weak one (reverse iamb)

verse   poetry

weak (or 'feminine') ending   a line of poetry with an extra, unstressed final syllable

Further reading

Three works of literary criticism

Laurie Maguire, *A Beginner's Guide to Shakespeare, Blackwell,* 2003

For a 'beginner's guide' this is quite challenging, but the short section on *Hamlet* offers some new ways to think about the play and is particularly good on the significance of historical context.

Michael Mangan, *A Preface to Shakespeare's Tragedies,* Longman, 1991

This is a book aimed at university students, but it is worth trying to read at least some of the chapter on *Hamlet* because it is packed with interesting interpretations.

Tony Tanner's Introduction to *William Shakespeare Tragedies (Volume 1): Hamlet, Othello, Macbeth, King Lear,* Everyman, 1992

Clearly written, Tanner provides a sensible and traditional introduction to *Hamlet*.

Useful websites

rsc.org.uk (Royal Shakespeare Company)

Simply searching for 'Hamlet' calls up a huge range of helpful articles, from a plot synopsis to trailers for the latest production. Even more helpful, you will find summaries of many different productions from over the years. Looking more widely, there is useful and clearly presented material on Shakespeare himself and the theatre in his lifetime.

bl.uk (British Library)

This has a huge Shakespeare section (bl.uk/shakespeare) with lots of clear and well-designed material. Searching for 'Hamlet' will bring up numerous articles, including one about 'gender and madness' in the play.

OXFORD
UNIVERSITY PRESS

Great Clarendon Street, Oxford, OX2 6DP,
United Kingdom

Oxford University Press is a department of the
University of Oxford. It furthers the University's
objective of excellence in research, scholarship,
and education by publishing worldwide. Oxford is a
registered trade mark of Oxford University Press in the
UK and in certain other countries

British Library Cataloguing in Publication Data

Data available

ISBN 978-019-839906-3

Kindle edition ISBN 978-019-839907-0

10 9 8 7 6 5 4 3 2 1

Printed in Great Britain by CPI Group (UK) Ltd., Croydon
CR0 4YY

Acknowledgements
The publisher and authors would like to thank the
following for permission to use photographs and other
copyright material:

Cover: © Mark Owen/Trevillion Images

p7: Photostage; **p13:** NILS JORGENSEN/REX/
Shutterstock; **p18:** age fotostock/Superstock; **p22:** ©
Corbis/Getty Images; **p25:** Universal Images Group/
Superstock; **p34:** Lebrecht Music and Arts Photo Library
/ Alamy Stock Photo; **p37:** iStockphoto; **p40:** Donald
Cooper/REX/Shutterstock; **p42:** Photostage; **p43:**
Alastair Muir/REX/Shutterstock; **p47:** Geraint Lewis/
REX/Shutterstock; **p51:** Alastair Muir/REX/Shutterstock;
p56: Photostage; **p61:** Richard Villalon/Fotolia; **p62:**
Shutterstock; **p72:** Alastair Muir/REX/Shutterstock;
p76: Geraint Lewis / Alamy Stock Photo; **p78:** REX/
Shutterstock; **p83:** Photostage; **p84:** travelibUK/Alamy
Stock Photo; **p86:** SPUTNIK/Alamy Stock Photo; **p88:**
Peter Horree/Alamy Stock Photo; **p89:** AF archive/Alamy
Stock Photo; **pp92-93:** Photostage.

Extracts are from William Shakespeare: *Hamlet*, Oxford
School Shakespeare edited by Roma Gill (OUP, 2007)

We are grateful for permission to reprint the following
copyright texts:

Marjorie Garber: extract from *Shakespeare After All*
(Pantheon Books, 2004), copyright © Marjorie Garber
2004, reprinted by permission of Pantheon Books, a
n imprint of the Knopf Doubleday Publishing Group,
a division of Penguin Random House LLC. All rights
reserved.

Laurie Maguire: extract from *Studying Shakespeare:
A Guide to the Plays* (Blackwell, 2004), reprinted by
permission of Blackwell Publishers, John Wiley and
Sons Inc, via Copyright Clearance Center, Inc

Royal Shakespeare Company: extracts from notes
on website, www.rsc.org.uk

Keith Thomas: extract from *Religion and the Decline of
Magic* (Weidenfeld & Nicolson, 1997), copyright © Keith
Thomas 1971, reprinted by permission of The Orion
Publishing Group, London.

We have tried to trace and contact all copyright
holders before publication. If notified, the publishers
will be pleased to rectify any errors or omissions at the
earliest opportunity.